The Revenue Relation

ACHIEVE GROWTH WITH RECURRING REVENUE
IN YOUR ONLINE SMALL BUSINESS

Kristina Romero

Romero Media

Romero Media LLC

4960 S. Gilbert Rd. Ste. 1-114

Chandler, AZ 85249

www.romeromedia.org

Ordering Information:

Quantity sales. Special discounts are available on quantity purchases by corporations, associations, and others. For details, visit the website https://therevenuerelationship.com.

The Revenue Relationship/ Kristina Romero. —1st ed.

ISBN 979-8-9852372-1-4

Contents

Dedicated to my family.

We make a living by what we get.
We make a life by what we give.

—WINSTON CHURCHILL

CHAPTER 1

The Problem of More

THANKS TO A ONCE-IN-A-LIFETIME OPPORTUNITY, I presented my new business plan over Zoom to the influential business guru Seth Godin. After running my web agency for nearly six years, I was ready to pivot with a larger-than-life idea in a new market with a new target audience. The former dot com business executive paused as he processed my "new big plan for growth." I nervously awaited a response during the private coaching session with this world-renowned, best-selling author.

"Are you listening? Don't do it." He stated calmly.

My initial thought was that he mustn't have understood me. In careful generalities, I had just laid out how I would attempt to build a large funnel to seek more clients, which involved casting a wide net to a different target market to grow my business to something bigger and better. I wanted something more profitable in less time, so I was doing what I thought would get me there—more external sales, new clients, and a new product.

I took a deep breath and braced for what he would say next.

"What would happen if the only people you were allowed to sell to were your existing clients? Could you create more value for them?" *The Dip* author gently suggested not to focus on lead generation but to turn inward for growth.

"If you don't like your current clients, then find clients who are worth everything you can offer them," he encouraged as he peered through his signature glasses.

Was it that simple? Had I been focused in the wrong direction? I had spent months and notable investment on heading down this new approach. It would be hard to let go, but I knew he was right. At that time, I had a healthy list of existing clients currently paying me regularly to support their website. I was neglecting relationships with my existing audience for one I had yet to build.

I got off the call with a new resolve and put Mr. Godin's advice to good use. I knew it was the right advice and the best move. I could be more profitable by becoming more efficient, creative, and *helpful* to my existing clients.

After that call, I moved forward with a vengeance to focus on my core client list as Mr. Godin instructed and, in turn, ultimately *doubled* my revenue for the year. By applying that mindset shift to focus inward, my entire business changed.

A broken system and thought process

Over the past few years, I have coached numerous website freelancers and web agency owners on creating more recurring revenue in their businesses. When in private conversations with my students, I see the thought process that has a hold on our industry, "Lead generation is the key to growth."

Look at any advertisement about sales scrolling through social media. You'll see endless ads that claim to solve problems with the latest lead generation trick or sales outreach technique.

When I poll my community of students on what training they want more of, the top choice is always lead generation.

It's not unusual in this seemingly competitive business climate to feel a consistent nagging that you're not doing enough to outreach. Often this works against you as there's a fine line between being motivated and being scared into inaction.

So, what if you could take everything you've already built and improve it? What if the problem wasn't lead generation but making sure the products you created, the clients you serve, and the processes you run were more profitable and provided consistent revenue?

Take a moment to reflect on your business, revenue, and expenses. What if you could keep the same sales but make more profit in less time? The answer lies in optimizing processes and creating recurring revenue products with what you already have in place. Once optimized, you're free to extend deeper into your business for opportunities that will then increase revenue.

This book will challenge you to turn inward, not outward. In these pages, you will find a philosophy, The Revenue Relationship. This philosophy is made practical through the CORE methodology (and its two sections CORE Calibration and CORE Revenue). The Revenue Relationship will help adjust your business to the new reality in the digital sales world. The pages in this book will help you focus on building a more resilient, reliable, and stable business so you can confidently face each day as a business owner.

The ideal business that is ready to turn inward

If you run a service-based business, then you regularly do something for someone else. Without even intending to, you've created transactional relationships. Serving others has also given you an existing client list where you can begin to dig deep to uncover something exceptional. If your business is struggling or unpredictable, it may be because you were told to focus outward for sales, not inward. Chances are you've missed out on opportunities staring you in the face.

I've worked extensively with small web agencies to turn inward, create recurring revenue, and develop a system for growth. Applying this methodology to other service-based businesses works because they share the same needs for growth. If you run a company that provides services to other small businesses, the methods, principles, and strategy I describe in this book will be perfect for you.

The best situation for businesses to apply these principles is those that provide services to other small businesses and can productize those services into recurring revenue products. Web agencies, web freelancers, marketers, consultants, coaches, financial services, and any other service-based business that provides other companies the tools for growth will benefit from what these chapters outline.

With the principles and strategies in this book, you'll discover the treasure you already have when you turn inward to your business and calibrate it to thrive!

The philosophy and methodology

After that fateful encounter with Seth Godin, my web agency grew exponentially. After some great years of growth, my systems and processes allowed me to sell my web agency due to the recurring revenue and value it possessed.

When preparing my web agency for sale, combing through my clients, revenue, and services, I made a startling discovery. That day of Seth Godin's advice did more than change my mindset. In applying his advice, I developed a philosophy for working with my clients. Subsequently, the execution of that philosophy created a methodology. I began to see I thrived when I valued relationships, and there was an inherent flow to the productized services I sold. I realized that my revenue supported my business in a way that made growth possible without a strong focus on new sales.

When I analyzed the last five years of my work as a web agency owner, The Revenue Relationship was born. Converting that philosophy practically led to crafting the CORE methodology.

The Revenue Relationship involves reframing your relationships with your client. I'll define The Revenue Relationship in depth in the next chapter. For now, I'll break down the CORE methodology that implements this philosophy.

The CORE methodology is designed to give you a system that will support the entire operation of your business.

CORE stands for Care (C), Optimize (O), Redesign (R), and Evolve (E).

CORE Calibration and CORE Revenue are ways we can apply the CORE methodology to build more recurring revenue. Recurring revenue is ongoing payments through subscriptions or memberships, typically productized services or digital products. When you set up CORE Revenue correctly, it can support all your business expenses, team salaries, your salary, business development, and outward lead generation.

A well-calibrated business with the CORE methodology at the center is a business that offers predictable monthly income, thrives without your 100% attention, and gives you more time and freedom to focus on the things you love.

The infographic below shows the CORE methodology and how each phase feeds into another. CORE Revenue consists of a Care product, Optimize product, Redesigns for clients, and evaluations that help them Evolve. A service-based business with this setup will produce enough from their CORE Revenue that it can reduce pressure for outward lead generation every month. We'll unpack this diagram more in the upcoming chapters.

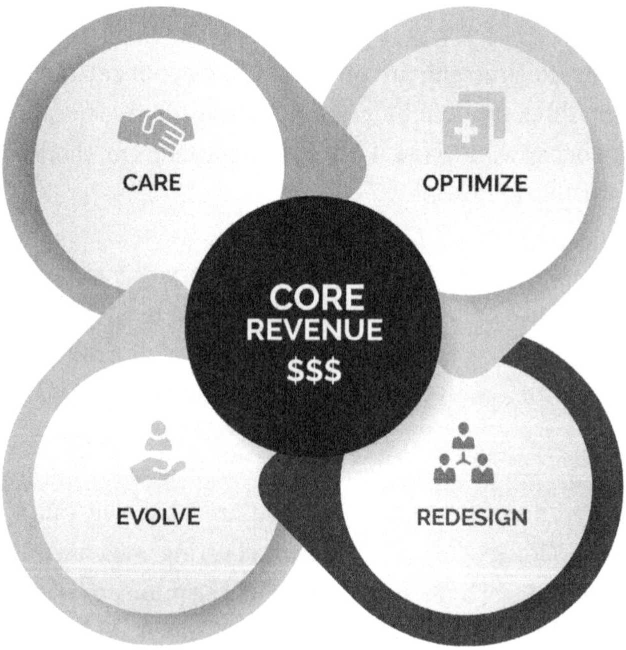

In the following chapters, I'll show you how to rework your business to apply The Revenue Relationship with CORE Calibration as well as build your CORE Revenue. These chapters will challenge the way you see your business. It will even challenge your role in your business, and that's the point. If we don't challenge ourselves to shift and adapt to what works, we'll never grow toward the goals we set for ourselves.

I can confidently say, The Revenue Relationship, executed through the CORE methodology, is the best way to secure long-term recurring revenue. What I also love about this approach is that it's a genuine and honest way to do business with clients. When you apply The Revenue Relationship, you shift focus from a lead generation money grab to serving your clients in a way that benefits both businesses. You'll find that recurring revenue is more satisfying when we serve our clients correctly, and the reward is business growth for all involved.

Throughout this book are examples of The Revenue Relationship in various business setups. In fact, there is an appendix at the end of the book that features examples of CORE applied to a wide range of industries. Towards the end of this book are action plans for executing the two main sections of the book: CORE Calibration and CORE Revenue.

Predictable monthly income is the holy grail, and I look forward to getting you to the chapters on the best way to do that, but we first need to do some housekeeping. To secure recurring revenue that will serve your business in the best way, we need to reframe our mindset for The Revenue Relationship.

CHAPTER 2

Defining The Revenue Relationship

"THE CUSTOMER IS ALWAYS RIGHT" WAS A PHILOSOPHY PIONEERED BY THE DEPARTMENT STORE RETAIL COMPANIES OF THE EARLY 1900S. Before then, customers had to worry about *caveat emptor* (let the buyer beware), a legal issue that if the buyer bought faulty goods, the blame was on them as consumers.

The new approach of "the customer is always right" removed buyer responsibility, and in turn, customers flocked to the stores that advertised this new policy. It also removed the fear associated with purchasing a defective or over-promised product.

Customer service models today aren't as straightforward. However, it helps to look at a contrasting view of "the customer is always right." One could argue the opposite view is that the customer knows nothing and can't make good decisions on their own. This philosophy comes across to customers that their buyer's journey is too complex to understand, they don't know what they want, and the seller will handle all the "tough stuff" for them. This approach only reassures buyers to a point. Once a customer gets burned, it creates massive distrust and paints a picture of a dubious industry.

For small service-based businesses that work directly with clients such as website designers, marketers, and online growth consultants, this pendulum of the two contrasting views have played out to create a real mess in their industry.

In digital agencies, "the customer is always right" with firm client-dictated digital services completely negates the expertise of the professional to the detriment of the project and the professional's business. Website professionals often burn out and suffer under this customer service model. They tend to undervalue their work and shrink away from suggesting services and products proactively that would encourage continuing relationships.

On the other hand, if digital agencies treat clients like they are ignorant and incapable of understanding aspects of the project, a misstep in the project creates immediate dissatisfaction. Once burned, clients resist due to a lack of trust, balk at high prices, and gravitate toward impersonal mass-market solutions that they can feel more in control over.

The best approach? The ideal spot for businesses that offer ongoing services and products is in the middle.

Between the pendulum of trusting the customer and the customer not trusting you is the customer trusting the decision you make because you are acting in *their* best interest. That is what I call The Revenue Relationship. The Revenue Relationship is the principle that customers and sellers invest in one another. The relationship is not simply transactional or based on one-off purchasing decisions. The Revenue Relationship is an ongoing transactional process that benefits both the seller and the buyer for continued growth.

When small business owners practice The Revenue Relationship philosophy, they communicate to the client that they learn and grow together. The investment is mutual. If the client invests in an ongoing relationship through a "care" product (which we will see in future chapters), the provider also invests in *them* through continual attention.

The death of the "transactional" relationship

In 2006, the year I learned HTML, simply having a website online met the customer's needs. Google was barely a household name, and Facebook was just two years old. Everything we know now about search engine and social media optimization didn't exist.

At that time, there wasn't much need for advanced inbound marketing, lead capture forms, or social media campaigns to drive traffic, sales, and trust among your target market. The web design industry, and much of online sales, was purely transactional.

The sales relationship with the client in 2006 was straightforward for a service-based digital agency. A client approached the web designer interested in a website. The web designer took the brief, created the deliverable, and closed the project.

There was no emphasis on the relationship between the web professional and client and if this pairing favored both parties. There was rarely a discussion of ROI or how this website would create a return over time.

We call this a "transactional" relationship. In this type of website design the transaction is payment for code and nothing more.

As the landscape of the internet, websites, and marketing changed, this transactional relationship model started to fail both the website professional and client. Why? Because the current ecosystem of the web industry started to demand different results. User experiences on websites and Google algorithms were changing.

This change required the client to seek further assistance and for the website professional to continue to educate and improve their skills to account for all these changes. Sticking with the transactional model left clients and professionals consistently finding new people once projects were over.

Over time I began to see that the transactional mindset was killing digital businesses. If website professionals wanted to stay in business, something needed to change. Trying to grow a business to adapt and change with the times is impossible if most of the week is spent searching for new potential clients.

The five principles of The Revenue Relationship

The solution to abandoning a transactional relationship with clients is to form a "revenue relationship." The Revenue Relationship is fundamental for anyone offering services in emerging markets like the online ecosystem. The growth of the internet has dramatically supported the motivation to transition to this business model.

As you shift your mindset toward this philosophy, five principles should frame the backbone of how you work with clients and promote your services and products online.

1. Put the business needs of the customer first

The Revenue Relationship is best applied to those who serve business owners. That is because your services have the potential of financially benefitting your clients. Only when a client has a business they need to grow can there be *revenue* in the relationship. Therefore, in this perspective, everything you do for businesses is focused on producing more income for their business.

By putting the client's business needs first instead of the deliverables, you're putting their business growth in the spotlight. That way, there is an expectation that investing in your services will directly or indirectly lead to their revenue growth.

Let's take website design and development as an example. In practical terms, instead of leading the conversation with the budget, the process should first involve what the website should achieve for the client's business. We then know if a budget specified is appropriate for those needs. Going with a results-focused approach is hard for web professionals who doubt their ability to achieve specific outcomes, but that's where transparency is essential. It doesn't mean you need to be an expert on everything, just that you work with the right clients at the right stage of your business.

2. Offer your customers E.A.T: Expertise, Authority, and Trustworthiness

In 2014 Google published guidelines for rating websites and introduced a principle known as E.A.T - Expertise, Authority, and Trust. We can apply that same guide to working with our clients.

In whatever you sell, you should first offer a solution to a problem as an expert. Educate yourself on the issues of your target audience. All your services or products should help your clients get past a hurdle. Become an expert on those hurdles.

When pitching solutions, do so from a place of authority because of your experience. Realize that each time you do a project, you are building that authority.

Trustworthiness shines through in how you show you help others, whether on your website, in case studies, or in testimonials. Trust builds as you communicate and follow through in each stage of your working relationship.

A website professional who practices The Revenue Relationship will often suggest discovery phases for clients to clarify their needs, evaluations to ensure they are hitting their goals, and products and services that help achieve results, rather than just "deliverables." The value you offer as an expert and authority who knows how to implement what they suggest is more valuable than any isolated designer or developer who provides websites in a one-off transaction.

3. Build on top of a recurring revenue product

The focus of The Revenue Relationship is that client work is an ongoing relationship, which is why this philosophy naturally pairs with creating recurring revenue. Recurring revenue makes your business resilient in times of feast and famine. Recurring revenue is the predictable revenue you are chasing to operate a profitable business.

We will get to creating a recurring revenue product in an upcoming chapter on constructing a "care" product. However, before we get to the *what*, let's discuss the *why*.

The recurring revenue you receive from the customer should be just as helpful to the client as it is to *your* bottom line. That's what the "relationship" part is all about. Recurring revenue needs to exist for their business to grow and for you to continue your growth of expertise and authority.

An easy recurring revenue product for many small businesses is simply productizing repeatable services into a monthly subscription. In digital agencies, these subscriptions position themselves as "monthly support." This support could be for the technology, the client, or both. It speaks to the "relational" portion - that you will be there for the client on an ongoing basis.

The first recurring revenue product you should build is a "care" product. The Care product offers that baseline support for your client, and it will be the gateway to your Revenue Relationship.

Does it work for all clients? No, that is why I will explore in the next chapter if your clients are the right clients for you. If you practice The Revenue Relationship, clients who refuse to engage in a recurring revenue subscription will be a red flag, a way to weed out the wrong clients for your business.

We will go over in detail how to create your Care product, how it serves as the gateway to a Revenue Relationship, and why it's the key to CORE Revenue in an upcoming chapter.

4. Believe businesses are living, breathing entities that must change over time

We've touched upon how the internet has changed. Any small business that engages in transactions on the internet is also subject to that fluidity. Your client who sells dog food online can't expect the same flow of revenue over ten years if their business hasn't adapted to the changes in e-commerce, social media marketing, and logistics.

It's a strong possibility that a website built today will be outdated in design and functionality in two years. A lead capture form that converted customers one year ago may seem pesky and annoying today. A design quickly becomes "so-2015," and once popular keywords can cease to help you rank on the first page of results.

The Revenue Relationship accounts for these changes. Whether it's online marketing tools like building websites or any service impacted by changing technology, always make your clients aware you are solving their problem for today, and the solution may need adjustment over time.

Business owners need to keep up-to-date and on top of major shifts in the markets. That can be challenging. It's hard to predict how the economy, internet, stock market, government regulations, or pandemics will change industries.

All you can offer is a Revenue Relationship that encourages a continued connection to provide solutions on an ongoing basis as these changes happen. In short, if your client is investing in you by engaging with an ongoing Care product, you will keep them top of mind.

5. View every transaction as an investment for both parties

It's easy to think of business as a series of transactions. You offer a service, and the client buys it because they need it. You exchange time for money and then continue in opposite directions. Yet, what happens when you need to invest in education, improve skillsets, or pivot in a new direction because of changes in the industry?

Service-based businesses struggle to thrive when viewed as a series of transactions because they must keep adapting to changes and shifting when solutions are not meeting the problems they once were. By your clients choosing to support you regularly through a recurring revenue product, they are also investing in your business. Conversely, by taking them on as a client, you too should be viewing that as investing in them.

Your products and services should be investments in their growth. Whatever you are offering should indeed be helping them achieve their goals. In this way, the investment is mutual.

For the web design industry, once clients hire you to work on their website, they are not just asking you for a website. Knowingly or unknowingly, they are asking you to be their expert. By working together on the initial website build, they begin to trust you.

Even if you don't want to continue support after the website has launched, they still have your email, whether you like it or not. Clients who see you as an expert will continue asking you for your insight and support until you break that trust or send them elsewhere. For that reason, agreeing to work with someone means investing in *them* as clients, so choose your clients wisely.

The Revenue Relationship keeps both parties in business

Restructuring to practice The Revenue Relationship will require more from you as a business owner. However, your work will pay off in a list of loyal clients and a more resilient business.

In turn, working with businesses that practice The Revenue Relationship is more attractive for your clients than the old “the customer is always right." You are not just doing what they request but partnering with them to reach a series of goals.

The Revenue Relationship asks more of you. It means you must further your education to help your clients achieve results. It also means you should be good at client-facing interactions, and if not, have someone on your team who is.

Those who practice The Revenue Relationship find that shifts in their industry don't concern them. They are prepared to pivot with those trends thanks to ongoing revenue from their client base they can use for education, business growth, hiring team members, or investing in software. With this mindset, you can be more resilient in troubling times.

Shifting your mindset isn't easy, and it may not happen overnight. To practically apply The Revenue Relationship mindset, you need to calibrate your business model to be ready for this change. Executing this shift through CORE Calibration is what we will explore in the following chapters.

CHAPTER 3

CORE Calibration: Care

THIS BOOK'S MAIN TWO SECTIONS FOR APPLYING THE REVENUE RELATIONSHIP ARE CORE CALIBRATION AND CORE REVENUE. CORE Calibration focuses on modifying your business so it can effectively create CORE Revenue. CORE Revenue is the four-step cycle of growing your clients with recurring revenue and additional services.

Each section has a step-by-step action plan at the back of the book. The action plan pairs with a printable PDF workbook available for download at therevenuerelationship.com. These CORE Action Plans contain questions and prompts to help you apply the elements of CORE Calibration and CORE Revenue to your business.

It's tempting to jump ahead and get right to the goods of creating more revenue with the CORE Revenue framework. However, it's counterproductive to learn how to build with CORE (Care, Optimize, Redesign, and Evolve) unless you have positioned your business in a way to adopt that methodology. That is what calibration is all about.

The CORE acronym is broken down as the C representing Care, O representing Optimize, R representing Redesign, and E representing Evolve.

These next four chapters will explore how Care, Optimize, Redesign, and Evolve apply to your specific business.

To calibrate your business, you will focus first on making sure you are focused on Care as a vital aspect of who you work with, what you offer, and how you deliver it. Then you'll Optimize by dialing into your processes to become more efficient and thus more profitable. Redesign will concentrate on redefining your role in your business and what you do day to day. Then Evolve challenges you to take your business to the next level as you assess what's working and what isn't working. After calibrating your business for the CORE methodology, you can build your CORE Revenue.

Both CORE Calibration and CORE Revenue are a circular system of four phases and can be customized. Knowing that may help you rework these to your business, products, services, and niche for optimal execution. All strategies, processes, and principles work best when tweaked to your specific industry.

Putting Care at the center

The foundational principle for the CORE methodology is putting Care at the center of your business. That means flipping your expectation that lead generation and marketing are the center of growth and moving toward focusing on the clients that you already have.

It doesn't matter how many clients you have or if you are just getting started. Applying CORE at any stage will secure habits and processes that attract more business.

As we discussed in the last chapter on The Revenue Relationship, putting Care at the center of your business doesn't mean putting your client at the center of your business. It means that you invest in your client's success, producing products and services that create success for them. In this case, the saying from John F. Kennedy, "A rising tide lifts all boats" is more applicable. If you focus on the rising success of your client base, you too will benefit from that success if you have the right revenue relationship.

Care is not customer first

The issue we have in discussing "care" is that Care can mean many different things to different people. If you calibrate your business to make Care the center, we need to get specific about what that implies.

The Cambridge Dictionary definition of care is "the process of protecting someone or something and providing what that person or thing needs." Care comes from the Latin *curo*, which helps define care as "to arrange, take care of, attend to."

When we serve the basic needs of our clients, we demonstrate care within this definition. Let's dig into how a company can calibrate itself to exhibit Care as a foundational principle.

1. Goal-driven results

What are the steps potential clients take to reach out to you? In your initial conversations with them, how do you position your company? When a potential client decides, why are they choosing you?

Too often, the budget takes front and center with new leads. It's the old transaction mindset that the commodity or deliverable is all that matters. This budget-only approach to conversations with potential clients focuses entirely on the wrong thing.

The entire relationship with the client needs to base itself on the results the client needs. Before speaking with a client on the phone, get them to think about their goals with an intake form. Doing so beforehand will allow the client the time to think through what success means to them.

Encouraging Care can be exhibited in the copy on your website, in an intake form, or in a follow-up email. If it's explained in the copy on your website, you need to list the main goals for most of your clients and then translate those into statements that will resonate with the potential client.

Suppose you are a website professional that puts Care at the center of your business. In that case, your intake inquiry form will ask about needs and goals (not just budget and features). You'll supply your clients with ongoing website care plans and continue to build your skills to deliver products and services that achieve common goals like social media optimization, social media management, or content creation.

If you are sending emails before a purchase decision, reiterate their goals back to them. Using the terms and phrases the client used helps you frame that these are the center of your working relationship.

All clients want are results. If you put their goals first, you are putting the success of their company at the center rather than deliverables.

2. Value Touchpoints

Touchpoints are the moments throughout a buyer's journey or a project where you reach out to the client. These can be emails, phone calls, text messages, or good old-fashioned snail mail.

When you are calibrating your business to put Care at the center, value touchpoints become a way to show your clients that you are willing to offer them information even if there is no transactional result to your outreach.

E-newsletters or running webinars for your clients are typical value touchpoints for many digital agencies. These forms of outreach focus on bringing value through education and, in turn, help position you to your client.

Other value touchpoints include emails sharing special deals you've found they may like, resources, or news stories that apply to them. In addition, you can send an email or text message on their birthday or a "welcome" packet in the mail when they start a project.

I've always admired home realtors and their long-term dedication to value touchpoints. Here in the US, realtors will send magazines, housewarming gifts, or text messages on your home-buying anniversary. They hope these touchpoints will keep them top of mind for referrals or even reselling the home you purchased with them, even though this could be ten years in the future!

Value touchpoints can be an excellent catalyst for continued investment and growth as they encourage referrals. They can be an instrument of education and lead to your client's investment in another product or service. Value touchpoints can also be a great way to announce pivots to new services, a natural step as they adapt and change.

Value touchpoints aren't about directly wanting something from the client or being motivated by a transactional outcome. It's what you do as a business who has Care at the center. Value touchpoints lead to increased revenue as they remind your clients of what you do and the focus you have on their goals.

3. Accessible

Businesses that want to calibrate for Care are accessible. That does not mean clients have your phone number and call you whenever they want. It's the opposite. Being accessible is about finding sustainable ways to support your clients, then setting the boundaries, so everyone knows the communication rules.

Accessible businesses encourage their clients to send requests, issues, or concerns; however, this does not mean you are there to address them immediately. If you offer continued support, invest in a support desk, even if it's just you or a small team. Customers have satisfaction emailing directly and receiving an auto-email to confirm the request was received. It keeps emails out of your inbox and helps position the mindset their ticket will take time to address.

Being accessible may also mean hiring a team or expanding your team so your company has the resources it needs to care for your clients properly. This calibration element is often left as the last step when a business owner is overburdened. A team member skilled in client communication can be a solid asset for your company, continue the relationship structure you built, and focus on providing the ongoing support your clients need.

4. Processes with boundaries for healthy relationships

As mentioned, putting Care at the center does not mean that the customer is the focus, only that the client's business needs and goals are the focus. That is hard to do when the client doesn't understand your boundaries and systems.

Clients are known to call outside of office hours, propose weekend work, send excessive emails, or nag about items that do not play into the success or growth of the business. Like in your personal life, you need boundaries for healthy relationships.

Calibrate your business to include working hours and stick to them. Many people come to expect that companies run a typical 9-5. However, many business owners will operate outside this time for various reasons.

For many years, my work hours were from 9 am – 1 pm. I only took calls from clients between 10 am - 12 pm on Mondays, Wednesdays, and Fridays. I found clients comply with the boundaries of work hours, but you are responsible for implementing them. Those that don't adhere often don't respect other boundaries. Crossing one boundary can be a red flag and may be a sign they are the wrong type of client, one in which you don't want a relationship.

To set communication hours, leverage a calendar booking system to allow only certain times of day for phone calls. That will enable you to spend less time defending your hours in an email and present a matter-of-fact step to speaking with you. When the client requests a call, send a simple link with "book in a time that works best for you."

If a client contacts you during off hours with texts to chat or emails that say, "Call me," set up automatic replies in various areas that remind your clients you don't respond during off hours. Train them to email your support desk, then provide procedures in your auto replies of what to do in case of emergencies.

5. Products and services that reflect principles

As you work the Care principle into your business, you need to look at the products and services you offer and ensure they reflect your new relationship outlook.

When discussing CORE Revenue in upcoming chapters, we will get into the specifics of creating a recurring revenue product. For now, you need to evaluate what you already have. It's worth looking back on your products and services and seeing if anything needs to be adjusted when operating in this new relationship mindset.

Often service-based businesses will fashion what they do based on something a client asked for, whether they offered it or not. That is never the best motivation for the creation of a service or product since it's a response to a transaction. Its only factor for existence was to win the bid.

The result is a mix of dissimilar types of clients and various kinds of products and services. Chances are you have a lot of great clients and desirable services that are working well for your business, but other clients and services are dragging it all down.

Now is the time to go back to those products and services and weed out what is costing you more energy than it should. Evaluate if a particular service is needed to benefit your clients' goals. A simple way to do this is to observe what takes you away from your clients whose businesses you could help grow. Specifically, suppose you are a marketing agency offering print design but finding this service is taking away valuable resources from 80% of your clients who only advertise online. In that case, the service may be doing more damage than good.

Another way to observe this is by looking at the balance sheet and what is not profitable. Products and services that are not profitable end up costing your clients because it's draining the financial resources you could use to grow your company to serve them better.

Observing whether to nix a product or service based on profitability is timely because, in the next chapter Optimize, we'll look specifically at making services more profitable. Many times, it's a process tweak or a scope of work fix. However, some services may be sucking away your time as the business owner more than it should. These can be eliminated or just better Optimized, as you'll see in the next chapter.

Lastly and most importantly, do your current suite of services and products suit the needs or goals of your customers? That is the biggest question to address, and it likely requires you to rework some of the current offerings to serve a specific niche of clients better.

Don't feel you need to get too caught up in this step right now for Care. Just note the principle as it applies to perfecting your offerings. The next chapter will explore that more and help you recognize what to prune, eliminate, or remake.

6. Products and services that form building blocks

In addition to editing your offerings, you must consider how they work together to help clients reach their goals. Many products or services offered by companies are disjointed, serve too many markets, and confuse the clients about what your business does.

To try and boil it down to a specific diagnosis, ask yourself, "Do my products or services connect to form building blocks toward specific goals?" Many people think of a buyer's journey before the purchase, but for The Revenue Relationship and CORE calibrated businesses, there's a buyer journey *after* the purchase. The whole idea of CORE Revenue is that it allows your clients to continue a buyer's journey even *after* an initial project is complete.

Take a good look at what you offer and evaluate whether it supports this ongoing buyer's journey to existing clients or if it's all positioned just for new leads. Do various services build on top of one another or do they feel siloed in their own universe?

All of what we will explore in the CORE methodology means nothing if you don't view a recurring revenue relationship as something valuable. Products and services that don't work together for recurring revenue will only lead to more one-off transactional relationships. If your offerings are all over the place, executing this shift will feel awkward. However, it's worth the work to change that. You aren't reading this book to stay stuck in one-off transactions but to grow your recurring revenue streams and make your business profitable.

Knowing who you serve

Calibrating your business to put Care at the center is a big adjustment. To achieve a mindset shift, you'll need to understand your ideal customer, rearrange services and products, and map out common client goals to know who you serve.

If you're feeling overwhelmed, it could be that you are not clear on who you serve best. Understanding your "niche" or target market is a great way to simplify how you apply Care to your business.

One practical tip to dialing in on your niche is evaluating past clients and projects for whom you enjoyed working with or helped succeed. In the next chapter, we'll discuss other tips for finding a niche if you don't have one. Nevertheless, dialing in on Care can be an easy way to find one. By taking a moment to evaluate the types of people or businesses you can help the most, you naturally form a segment of buyers.

As we wrap up this element, focus on taking what you have already built and tweaking the areas you can incorporate the Care aspect of the CORE methodology. With Care better explained, let's move on to how you Optimize your business with CORE Calibration.

CHAPTER 4

CORE Calibration: Optimize

NOW THAT YOU'VE CALIBRATED YOUR BUSINESS TO PUT CARE AT THE CENTER (C IN CORE), IT'S TIME TO TURN TO OPTIMIZING (O IN CORE). Inside CORE Calibration, Optimize means improving processes to create more profit. You can earn more profit from the same amount of sales when you reduce the time to execute (through adding in support or automation) or fine-tuning what you offer.

Whether you are the only employee or an entire team, you must continually optimize your business to the point of a well-oiled machine. That can be a challenge if there are no processes in place, products and services don't complement each other, and the scope of work changes with each customer.

This chapter will outline the steps to optimize your business systematically. Eventually, at the end of this book you'll dig into these concepts and how they apply to you in the CORE Action Plans.

Focus your efforts by remembering your niche

Before we begin on the key elements of optimizing your business, we should step back to the starting line by discussing who you serve best. We touched up on this at the end of the last chapter. Knowing your ideal client gives you the power to make decisions. If you find limiting your services, editing your offerings, or optimizing processes challenging, you may need to run through some exercises to clarify your niche.

What exactly is a niche? In the broadest sense, it's not a single industry but a segment of buyers who share common traits. The misconception is to think of it as a category or an age demographic when it is just a profile of buyers.

A "niche" can be a combination of a person, place, and thing. For example, serving Los Angeles fitness coaches with membership websites is a well-defined niche consisting of a type of person, location, and technology (or thing).

Some niches can be businesses operating at a stage in their business, like "small local business owners with an internal team of 5 or less." Specific niches like "product creators with e-stores who make 1MM" or "mid-size businesses with an internal email list of 5K subscribers" are focused on a stage because the service provider is confident they can take them to the next level.

Optimizing starts with knowing what it is you do and who you serve. As you optimize in the areas below, ask yourself, "Does this serve my niche?" Boundaries you create, services you offer, or processes in place may make targeting your niche more difficult.

Specifically, if you serve aspiring entrepreneurs looking to leave their full-time job, optimizing your business to only book calls on weekdays from 9 am - 5 pm may work against this niche since they work full-time. You may decide your days off will be Sunday and Monday, so you can open slots on Saturdays for client meetings since your clients work full-time jobs during the week.

There's no need to decide your niche before this chapter is over. You'll have time to work on that in the action plans provided at the end of this book.

Now with keeping a niche in mind, I will focus on two main areas for optimization: processes and staff.

1. Services need a well-defined scope of work

Profit arises from knowing and anticipating the time and resources that go into your services. If you offer a productized service for $100 a month, $50 in expenses in time to execute is steep. However, if you reduce the time by half to better optimize the process, you increase the profit. With optimization, you can turn that $ 50-a-month profit into $75. That is why processes are critical. You must have a process for the productized service to determine its profitability.

As we'll see in the upcoming CORE Revenue section, productized services are the key to recurring revenue for service-based businesses. However, it's more than productized services that need well-defined scopes of work. Everything you offer needs a process, and for anything to have a process, it first needs to have a well-defined scope of work.

An SOW, or scope of work, creates boundaries around what you offer and anticipates the time involved in executing. Setting up a scope of work for everything you offer doesn't mean you remove the freedom to change, adapt, or add on. SOWs help you set expectations for yourself and your client.

Setting a scope of work allows you to also add exceptions for unexpected variations. For example, if you offer a one-hour service to evaluate a website for security flaws, have your process take 30 minutes, leaving an extra 30 minutes for the unknown. Not all websites are the same, and different issues arise, so you include that additional 30 minutes in the scope for underlying problems. The time restraint of one hour offers a nice boundary for your team with the freedom to address variables. Anything that creeps up over one hour becomes "out of scope" and allows you to charge the client based on this change.

If creating fixed scopes of work is challenging, return to who you serve best. To optimize your business better, define if your services' scope of work benefits your niche. If your services are all over the place, the types of clients you serve may be too.

You will not be profitable if you continually shift what you offer for each client and project. It is best if you have a set scope of work to create recurring revenue products (which will be defined later in CORE Revenue). However, a firm scope of work even applies to quoting out projects and proposals for one-off solutions.

When quoting out projects, you want to craft your proposal with a series of deliverables, stages, and actions that build on top of one another. Challenge yourself to only offer well-defined services with clear boundaries for what they include. Scope creep is the number one killer of profit in service-based businesses, and it can be avoided by simply defining each line item's scope of work. It can be tedious and time-consuming at first, but it saves you time and money in the long run.

2. Processes need to exist for everything you offer

As explained in the last point, processes can only be assigned if there's a well-defined scope of work. However, when you sit down to write a checklist or workflow for everything you offer, you may realize some services present a challenge creating a straightforward process. That could be a problem. If you find it impossible for there to be a process or a well-defined scope of work, you may need to eliminate this offering in your business.

That seems harsh, but there's a good reason. You cannot outsource anything that doesn't have a process. That means the business must rely on you for every step of this offering. Even if you hand it off to another team member, a lack of a process or scope of work hinders quality assurance. Your team member is blamed for a failure of execution when it was really the lack of a process.

The good news? Most offerings can find a process. The simple rule is: if it's repeatable, it can be a process. If it's a process, then it can be delegated. If it can be delegated, it can be profitable.

Now, processes apply to more than just the actual execution of a project. Onboarding and offboarding processes are just as important. When you have solid onboarding and offboarding processes, everything you offer has the flexibility and room for variables depending on who you serve. Onboarding processes are a great way to eliminate many variables and ensure all clients start on the same level.

For example, an online marketing agency that offers search engine optimization services finds Business A and Business B both require monthly SEO. However, if Business A doesn't have its website ready for SEO because of a series of checklist items, the agency can't apply the same process to both. The online marketing company could offer a "kicking off" service or paid onboarding product. In that case, this will allow Business A to arrive at the same level as Business B and the process for monthly SEO services to be the same for both.

3. Automate, delegate, or reassign for productivity

When you look inward at what you do and do well, you may find many of those hours sucked up by bottleneck tasks and administration work that takes you away from business growth. In the next chapter, we will dig deeper into your role to discover how to redesign the way your role functions. For now, we'll focus strictly on productivity.

Your role should not bottleneck. Work on avoiding micromanaging or overcorrecting according to your preferences. In the same way, your team members should also avoid bottlenecking essential steps in a process.

As you iron out your processes for both services and productized services, look for which tasks prevent smooth execution and costs you profit. Review all the processes from onboarding, execution, and offboarding, to find points where the flow is blocked by either a task or the need for your personal input.

You are the most expensive person in your business. Every moment you spend during the execution of a process is the highest-paid person in your business executing that step. When you can remove yourself from the day-to-day tasks, business processes, or even admin tasks, you are essentially creating profit in your business.

That plays directly into growth. You can't grow your business if you are stuck inside daily tasks that can be automated or delegated to someone else. When you're bogged down with tasks that don't need to involve you, you sacrifice The Revenue Relationship. Your clients benefit greatly when you're free to grow the business and offer them better and more effective solutions, not when you're buried up to your eyeballs in work that is better delegated, eliminated, or automated.

One way to free yourself from bottlenecks is automation. Automating processes doesn't need to be as complex as it sounds. Automating can be a canned email reply that takes five seconds to paste versus the usual five minutes to write. Automation is also using a support desk SaaS with a ticketing system that let clients know their request has been received. Automating takes the repeatable moments of the process and has a way of triggering a step without the need for human interaction.

Automating can get fancy when you look at incorporating specific software like Zapier. With online automation software, you can combine different pieces to trigger entire processes. One of my favorite automation sequences is my booking calendar, which can gather all the information I need for a meeting, create the calendar invite, and set up the virtual meeting room. The sequence will then send email reminders to the client and anything else they need to know. Yes, it is simple out-of-the-box functionality of most online booking systems, and that's the point. Automation should be simple, like a human process done a thousand times.

Processes thrive with automation if they help humans push through bottlenecks. However, I firmly believe that for a service-based business to stay successful, it still needs human interaction. As you delegate and reassign pieces of your action steps to the right seat in the company, remember automation is fluid. When processes fail, it's an opportunity to see where automation can be improved, removed, or reassigned to human staff.

As you delegate and reassign processes, realize that this is about removing bottlenecks. Have your team document their steps with a screencast, and you'll begin to see a pattern so you can improve and optimize for profit.

4. Your team's roles need to be well-defined

Now we come to optimizing your team's roles, and here's where many of us get into trouble. Often as our business grows and changes, we discover people are in the wrong seat, a job role is redundant, or a team member is not working out.

Just like the errors of accepting every client at the beginning of your business because of desperation, you can do the same with staff. Staff typically forms from a specific one-off need and finding someone specific to a skill set. Roles can get messy as your business grows, especially if you find your team needs a broader skill set.

There are two ways to approach this issue. One way is to regularly train your staff for skills as you expand your services. Invest in their training to evolve the person in their role. The other is to do the reverse: only accept projects that fit your staff's existing skill set rather than trying to change their skill sets to suit the work you take on.

I often see people attempt to create unicorn hires. A unicorn hire is someone who can work a wide variety of tasks and roles, like a content writer who can code and execute customer-facing email support.

There was a time early in my career when I was that unicorn hire. I did everything my boss needed: web design, copywriting, marital counseling, cleaning, getting the coffee, and reviewing reports. My position could have been as a web designer, a personal assistant, HR, and a janitor. My stress level was high, and I quickly left that job.

The issue with unicorn hires is that the role refuses to be defined because it has more than one clear objective. Therefore, it creates a cloud of confusion, which inevitably creates stress. We all know what happens when people are stressed: they quit. If quitting is not an option, the other alternative is to underperform.

If you experience high turnover or underperformers, you must look at the role to find the issue. Is the role well defined? Check the processes. Is everything they do a well-defined process? Can they look at their day and predict, within reason, what they will work on and their objectives?

If you don't know, ask them. Be open to honest feedback. Ask what your team members love about their job and what they hate about their job. Understanding what they love and hate about their role will help you better understand why they're performing well in certain areas and underperforming in others.

If what they hate about their role is essential to what they need to do for the business to thrive, you may need to create another position. If a separate team member is not an option for financial reasons or logistics, you must evaluate if they are still the right person for the job.

You should also factor in how much your team members make and if it's fair market pay. Underpaying fair market value will lead to high turnover. Pay people what they're worth, give them set processes, and encourage them to develop new skills. In turn, you will have loyal and happy team members.

Understanding your team members' roles is understanding your business's processes. It can be a lot of work to do what you need to do to understand this piece of your business. Yet, you need to pay attention to avoid losing revenue with high turnover, underperforming team members, and broken processes that don't serve your clients.

Staying focused on processes for profit

If you aren't optimizing your businesses by creating processes, you are your worst enemy. Often trying to fill in the gaps of what needs to be fixed by hiring someone, firing someone, buying a new tool, taking on more work, or adding on more services only makes it worse.

Do the work to craft the right products and services for your niche, optimize them with processes, and delegate them to team members whose roles are well defined. This way, your role becomes only tweaking a process *back* on track day-to-day.

Optimizing takes a lot of decisions, hard decisions. Once you've made them, you need to commit and follow through. Put Care at the center, then Optimize your business to grow so you can better service your list of clients.

CHAPTER 5

CORE Calibration: Redesign

To say life is full of pivotal moments is an understatement. The only thing we can predict about our business decisions is that, at some point, we will pivot. Redesigning our business for a more systematic approach is part of running a business.

In the last chapter, we reviewed ways to optimize, and optimization often requires reworking what exists. Optimization naturally progresses into redesigning, the step to take to revise your business where you want it to be.

A redesign can also mean "redefine" in this context. It may involve redefining service offerings, a role for someone on your team, or even redefining where you fit in the business now that it's grown.

Since redesigning your business is work only you can define, the best place to look for what to Redesign is your role. In this chapter, I will show how you can redefine your role to eliminate stress and love our businesses again.

Loving your business again

Burnout is normal. If you have yet to experience burnout, chances are you haven't been doing your role long enough. When becoming their own boss, people make false assumptions that they won't feel the same stress and burnout they did working "for the man." Sadly, this is not true. Often, we are a worse boss to ourselves!

Don't believe me? When was the last time you vacationed and didn't bring your computer? When was the last time you didn't think about work on the weekend? When was the last time your work hour stopped at five o'clock, and you didn't pick up the phone, check your email, or flip open the computer to do something "really quickly"?

We all need to Redesign our roles so we can be better bosses to ourselves. We all need to work a little better at closing the door on "business owner" for the day and resuming being a parent, a better partner, or even just a relaxed human being.

It's easy to point the finger at your clients or staff as the reason you are stressing out in your role. However, as the business owner, you are the one who creates the rhythm for your team, and you are the one setting (or not setting) the boundaries for your clients. Any stress you are feeling in your business is within your control.

To adjust, look at some critical points of Redesign for your role while calibrating your business to be Care focused.

1. Finding what it is you love to do

It's expected as an entrepreneur to initially build a business by wearing most of the hats. One moment you're the accountant, and the next, you're a graphic designer or sales rep. Wearing all the hats can give the feeling that you're in control. As the business grows, there's a temptation that relinquishing control to someone else will cause the business to fall apart. Often, this fear can keep you from doing what you love.

When you look at redesigning your role, the key phrase here is "redesign." It means that at some point, you did a task whether you liked it or not. It was necessary at some point and worked for that moment in the business. Now, however, it needs to be revisited, redesigned.

Think of this in terms of a business website. When a website client needs a new business website, often, they don't come prepared with the elements they need for the website to shine, like well-written copy or dynamic images. However, they need a live website to start generating business. After some time, the website will need to be redesigned, get well-written copy, dynamic images, and a new purpose altogether.

That is an excellent analogy for a business owner role in a company. You had to start somewhere, and you began with whatever you had. Then, as your business grew, you started to see things that you should have included in your role or something you included that you didn't need. Like a new business website no longer telling the story for a company after some time, your role may no longer reflect what you should be doing in your company.

So now, you must dig in, scrap what isn't working, keep the things that are working, and build off what you already started. That is why it's called Redesign, like a website redesign. Some pieces are going to stay, some delegated, and some eliminated. As discussed in the last chapter,

Optimize, some elements may be best for an automation tool to carry out or a third-party service.

If you need help figuring out where to start, the CORE Action Plans at the end of this book have you covered. A major task in that worksheet is taking a piece of paper and writing out everything you do during the day. After that exercise, you'll begin to see the things you do better fitted for somebody else.

Another way you can understand your role is to create a job description for yourself (also a task in the CORE Action Plans). When viewing everything you do inside a job description, ask yourself, "Would I apply for this job?"

The key to Redesign in CORE Calibration is to evaluate the parts of the job for the things you love to do. Those things will help your role shine because you will have to determine what is getting in the way of doing the things you love.

You are in complete control of your role, how others perceive it, and what it will look like moving forward. That's where we want to get to when calibrating our business with The Revenue Relationship. The goal is to keep intact the things that you love to do and the reason you started your company.

2. Find where you can remove yourself from a process

Not everything you need to eliminate from your role involves removing or hiring. Having a process involving automation is instrumental to creating a workflow that removes elements that don't need your attention.

To effectively delegate or automate, you need to go through the day and see ways to automate, outsource, and increase productivity to get more time and optimize your business.

A practical way to do this is by improving your email and communication situation. Leverage tagging, filters, and auto replies to ensure that whatever time you spend in your email inbox is significantly reduced. If you spend two hours on email daily, set a goal to get that down to one hour. Reroute emails from clients to support desk software, use saved canned email replies, and auto-filter emails to folders based on the sender or subject line.

Another practical method is to have a booking calendar. Designate specific times for meetings allowing the rest of the day to be free from the distraction of remembering if you have upcoming appointments. If you only allowed client calls from 9 am to 11 am Monday through Friday, you'll have a significant portion of the day to work on something else undistracted and uninterrupted. Generally, clients comply with these schedules, and you will find not having your day broken up with meetings improves the flow of productivity and focus.

3. Repositioning with your clients your new role

When you first interact with clients, you unknowingly paint a picture for them about what you do and how you will serve them. Sometimes their view of you gets locked in and difficult to reposition. By now, you've already thought of ideas to change your business as you focus on The Revenue Relationship. How will you present this to your clients to communicate the changes effectively?

Part of Redesign in CORE is repositioning how your clients see you in your role, how they see your team, how they see your business, and how they refer others to your business when speaking about what it is that you do.

In thinking of The Revenue Relationship, you should see that redesigning your business in the minds of your clients is all about playing into the mutual benefits you share in helping one another. Redesigning your role to your clients is easy when you include The Revenue Relationship. Remember, there is no need to explain why you are making the changes, only what is changing. They're only going to understand the modifications from their viewpoint and how it benefits them.

When reaching out to clients to reposition your new role or services, I suggest crafting from the approach I call "the reason for the change." When you send an email to your clients, you want to announce your new changes by positioning it as an announcement and something that benefits them.

Begin this email by stating what they are familiar with regarding your business.

> Dear Client,
> I've enjoyed your website design and development work for the past 10 years. **Then state the reason for the change.**
> As the business grows, I can now expand our offerings to include more services that will increase website traffic and user experience. **Then present the new changes and how this benefits them.**
> With expanding our offerings, I've hired two new team members to take over design and development, adding new SEO and content creation services to help grow your business.
>
> **If the change involves new boundaries, price changes, or protocol, add them next.**
> With these changes, I will no longer be the point person on projects. Instead, our new team will handle each piece of the builds from our project support desk.

Conclude with outlining any new procedures and excitement over this recent change.
All project requests, notes, and tasks should be sent to our support staff at support@myemailaddress.com, and you'll receive quick communication back for a better workflow!

If you are in the website industry, this email is something you send when you move from a freelancer to becoming a web agency with staff. The role shifts from a client-focused freelancer doing all the work to being a creative director and having people on your team executing the tasks. Any change in your working relationship with your clients requires a shift to how this can benefit them. For example, includes highlighting benefits like more attention, more skills on the team, faster turnaround, or a better product.

Besides initial outreach, you will also need to rework copy on your website, focusing on benefits. By redefining your role in the business with The Revenue Relationship, you can communicate how you appreciate your clients' loyalty and how you will, in turn, provide ways to grow their business.

As you embrace Redesign in CORE Calibration, take this opportunity to change how you work, your daily routine, and even your email signature to reflect this new outlook for your business.

4. Repositioning your business for new markets

I started this chapter by discussing pivoting. As you shift your mindset with The Revenue Relationship, you may find that redesigning your role means redesigning the company.

You are not scrapping your business and starting over. What you've learned in your business with your clients has better positioned you to be the business owner you are today. I've seen many business owners get burned out and want to scrap everything and pivot in a new direction. I wouldn't be serving Seth Godin's advice properly if I didn't point out that you have already done the work to help you effectively pivot.

Although your list may include clients that could be better, it is still a list of people who have proven that they will work with you. They have pulled out their credit card or their checkbooks and trusted you. That list is still a list of established relationships and the most vital asset for your company.

A client list is everything for a service-based business. When selling a service-based company, you're often selling a client list as the only valuable asset.

So, as you begin to redesign your business, not just your role, keep in mind that you should be client focused. If you want to pivot into different services, excellent. If you're going to shift into more productized services, even better. It may mean serving this client list in a completely different way. Whatever it is, focus first on your clients and your client goals as you redesign.

Keeping focused on the goals to execute

As you structure your businesses to put Care at the center, Optimize, and then Redesign, it's normal to feel overwhelmed by the number of changes required to execute.

Before I move on to our last step for calibrating your business with the CORE methodology, it's helpful to remember why you want to do this. Securing recurring revenue in your business allows you to be more resilient in times of trouble, to ease the burden of stress for your bottom line, and to create something that's going to grow over many years. To achieve this, you must change how you do things.

Dig back in and rework what you have already built to apply this methodology to structures that can sustain upcoming tactics for CORE Revenue. Implementing client-centered and client-focused business changes to accommodate The Revenue Relationship will allow you to make the right decisions for challenges that arise out of CORE Calibration.

The last step in calibrating your businesses with the CORE methodology is evaluating where you are so you can Evolve what you have to the next level. Before I venture into CORE Revenue to show you how to create products, optimize processes, and shift your working model completely, continue to the last step in CORE Calibration to tackle Evolve and what that means for your business.

CHAPTER 6

CORE Calibration: Evolve

EACH LETTER IN THE CORE METHODOLOGY BUILDS ON EACH OTHER FOR CALIBRATING YOUR BUSINESS TO ACHIEVE CORE REVENUE. It's only because of Care (C) that you can effectively Optimize (O). Only when optimizations are in place can we Redesign (R). It's only once we redesign can we move forward to the next stage - Evolve (E).

After you Evolve, you should expect to cycle again through all four stages as you grow. The Evolve phase will give insight to circle back to Care to tweak and perfect your products and services. Further optimizing those offerings, you then redesign your business to incorporate the changes. Then again, you'll need to evaluate to evolve to the next level before cycling again.

In short, CORE Calibration isn't a one-time process. The CORE methodology is a cycle to be applied to your business continuously. This cycle will mirror what you see in the upcoming chapters on

CORE Revenue which involves using the method to assist your clients' growth.

Evolving your business is dependent on you achieving a shifted perspective (Care), perfected processes (Optimize), and restructuring (Redesign). Although these are all good in theory, how do you properly evaluate to move forward to the next stage?

There are great books, course programs, and online social media gurus that can speak to various ways to take your business to the next level. In this chapter, I want you to keep your focus on the reason why you are evolving, The Revenue Relationship. When you're looking to evolve to the next level of your business, you're doing it with the mindset of serving your client list. That relationship aspect increases the recurring revenue and gives you the fuel to evolve.

In this chapter, we'll look at various circumstances and questions to help you take your business to the next level by evaluating what you have and where you can evolve it to be bigger, better, and stronger.

I'll caution you first by saying the push to be bigger and better may unintentionally create more work around things that don't matter. The busy work can make you feel like you're doing something when, in fact, you are on a treadmill going nowhere. I'm hoping you'll learn the difference.

We can experience this from our clients when we receive requests that won't get them to their goals. A web design client may send endless design notes about adding padding around paragraphs, and yet their copy is full of misspellings with unengaging copy that is too lengthy for anyone to read. What good are design tweaks if the substance isn't there? The client obsesses about the wrong things, dialing into insignificant details and missing the bigger picture.

We do the same when we evaluate our business in the wrong places. To evolve correctly, keep your focus on the larger goals you set for yourself. I'll start there: setting goals.

1. Know your numbers and focus on MRR

Monthly recurring revenue, or MRR, is essential to business growth and resiliency. It's just any recurring revenue. The best kind is MRR from a core client list that leads to more revenue in other areas of your business. That is the difference between product creators securing recurring revenue and service-based companies, like yours, securing recurring revenue.

When you focus on creating more MRR, you need to know your numbers around where your revenue comes from. Significant numbers include what additional revenue comes from that core client list of clients on a MRR productized service.

These MRR numbers will make more sense when I shift focus to CORE Revenue, but while here in Evolve (evaluating our business to take them to the next level), you want to know your numbers broken down by the source of the revenue.

Understanding how revenue is different is like understanding how food breaks down in the body. All carbohydrate-loaded foods don't break down the same. They break down in our bodies at different speeds. Eating an apple that is 25 carbohydrates may break slowly, giving you a particular type of energy over time, whereas eating a slice of bread that is also 25 carbohydrates breaks down quickly, producing a different result in your body. Even though they are the same amount of carbohydrates, the apple will give you more long-term energy than a slice of bread. We need to apply the same logic in terms of revenue.

If you're receiving $100 every month (MRR) from Client A for a productized service (a Care product), and because of that relationship, you eventually engage in a $10,000 project, that $100 MRR revenue is worth more to your business than just $100 a month. With this MRR relationship (a Care product) and a project for $10,000, you are further solidifying a relationship with that client that is going to continue to lead toward more revenue. They have proven to engage in additional revenue and established a relationship, thus proving more value than the MRR number indicates.

In contrast, if Client B came to you for a $10,000 project and then left and did not continue a relationship with you for a $ 100-a-month Care product, that $10,000 serves your business as a one-off transaction and does not further support the expectation of additional revenue from that client. Like the slice of bread, they burn up quickly with no chance of additional revenue.

The $10,000 from Client A and the $10,000 from Client B are two different revenue types. On your balance sheet, they look the same, but the quality and relationship of Client A make them way more valuable than Client B.

That is also why service-based businesses have more value if they sell their business with established MRR. A company that made $100,000 of one-off revenue for website development isn't the same value as a business that made $100,000 in recurring revenue.

Know your numbers as it relates to where the sources of that revenue are. When evaluating your financials, think about it through this lens, and you begin to see your clients in a brand-new light.

2. Set SMART goals for yourself, your team, and your clients

SMART goals are a popular exercise to keep you motivated and focused on what is essential. SMART is an acronym for specific, measurable, achievable, relevant, and time-bound.

The point of making SMART goals is to boil down what you want to achieve in a digestible way. When I talk about putting Care at the center of your business, it means thinking about SMART goals for yourself, your team, and your clients.

Your team members should understand what makes your businesses tick, what you're trying to achieve, and what role they play in the "grand plan." You'll want to encourage them to make SMART goals while understanding what they need to do to help move the needle for the business overall. Give them the power to help move the company forward in their role, and it will empower them to make suggestions.

Now, why create SMART goals for your clients? I'll get into that more within the CORE Revenue section, but in brief, SMART goals for your clients directly relate to creating more revenue in your business. When you focus on the SMART goals of your clients and what they are trying to achieve, you find ways to help them.

Set SMART goals for yourself with a focus on The Revenue Relationship. Will adding more clients increase your profit? That is the measurable piece of a SMART goal that is the most important.

We need to measure (the M in SMART) whether a particular project or client has been profitable to gauge whether increasing acquisition is fruitful or problematic. In Evolve, it's great to have a specific, achievable, relevant, and time-bound goal, but it's more important to measure the goal.

When you look at what you're doing to evaluate a goal of 20 more clients, $1000/m in MRR, or two more projects a month, what metrics are you using? What data points are you targeting? Is what you are trying to achieve profitable?

Invest in tools to help determine those things. Why work hard for more revenue, acquire more clients, or create more services if it's not profitable? When you measure your success, measure with an understanding that what you executed is profitable.

3. Invest in tools and the right financial help

In coaching business owners, I notice often, no one can quickly access their numbers. All this focus is put on increasing revenue, and yet most don't know their sales, expenses, or conversion percentages.

Many tools are available to track conversion, acquisition, revenue, and profit success, and yet, many of us need to spend more time or money to track this area of our business.

Now I'm generalizing here. Some people are very good at this and understand the importance, but this is a common trait among small business owners, so it's worth calling out.

In this instance, you can leverage automation to make this area of your business easier. There are various online software tools that can connect to create dashboards for yourself and measure KPIs (Key Performance Indicators). Measuring KPIs is an undervalued exercise for many small business owners. Yet, it's vital to your growth to be resilient and know which pieces of your business you need to grow, prune, or eliminate.

As I discuss this step inside the CORE methodology, Evolve in a business is meant to help make it more profitable. The only way to understand what makes you profitable is to understand your numbers, and you need the tools and the right financial help to do that.

Most people reading this book will be small business owners with a few team members if any. So, the help you're looking for is a bookkeeper, an accountant, and a payroll service. Regarding tools, you can look for a database system that tracks sales to filter and view based on conditions. Also helpful is a CRM, a customer relationship management tool, that allows you to tag your clients with different tags so you can create KPI dashboards.

A KPI dashboard can show you how many leads have converted, how many customers are in a recurring revenue subscription, how many projects are active, and so forth. Your accountant or bookkeeper should have a dashboard that shows you your total revenue compared to your expenses and your net profit. Have your bookkeeper create different groups for your different types of revenue based on where it comes from your CORE Revenue (existing clients) or a new client.

When looking at dashboards and reports, focus on quarterly goals and execute your changes within those boundaries. Setting goals by financial quarters makes execution manageable. When charting your goals and focusing quarterly, you can handle the steps you need to execute to reach large targets. Leverage the tools and the right help to financially get a good perspective on your company so you can evolve.

Evolving by evaluating

The only way to evolve our business to the next level is to evaluate what's working. Evaluation also motivates us to change. Implementing change is hard work, and not everybody is up for the task.

I'm surprised how many people have good intentions about making changes but don't. It is often overwhelm, not indifference, holding people back. Just putting in a tiny effort to evaluate will motivate you to do more. Start with your MRR productized services. Once you know a productized service isn't profitable, you're forced to change it. That knowledge is the driver to Evolve.

Evaluating your business is an ongoing exercise within the CORE methodology. You need ongoing reports to get the ten-thousand-foot view. Then you need to come back down from that ten-thousand-foot view and single out the things you need to execute in Care, Optimize, and Redesign. With the proper tools, you can get that down to an hour a week.

When you evaluate what's working and profitable, you can take that information to evolve your business to the next level and complete the initial cycle of the CORE methodology. With that final piece, your business will properly calibrate, and you'll be ready to create CORE Revenue.

CHAPTER 7

CORE Revenue: Care

NOW THAT WE'VE ADEQUATELY CALIBRATED OUR BUSINESS TO INCORPORATE THE REVENUE RELATIONSHIP, it's time to turn to building the revenue you need for sustainability. I call this type of revenue CORE Revenue. CORE Revenue is the secret sauce to everything I've been exploring. It's CORE Revenue that allows you to place a value on your business, have a loyal list of clients, and support your company's continued growth.

Like a wheel on a car, CORE revenue is the hub and includes all the revenue from your CORE list of clients. The spokes on that wheel supported by that hub are team or outsourcing expenses, software expenses, marketing and lead generation, and business admin expenses like your salary. The recurring revenue from that CORE list makes the wheel turn, supporting the other areas of the business.

See how CORE Revenue supports the areas of a digital web agency in the diagram below:

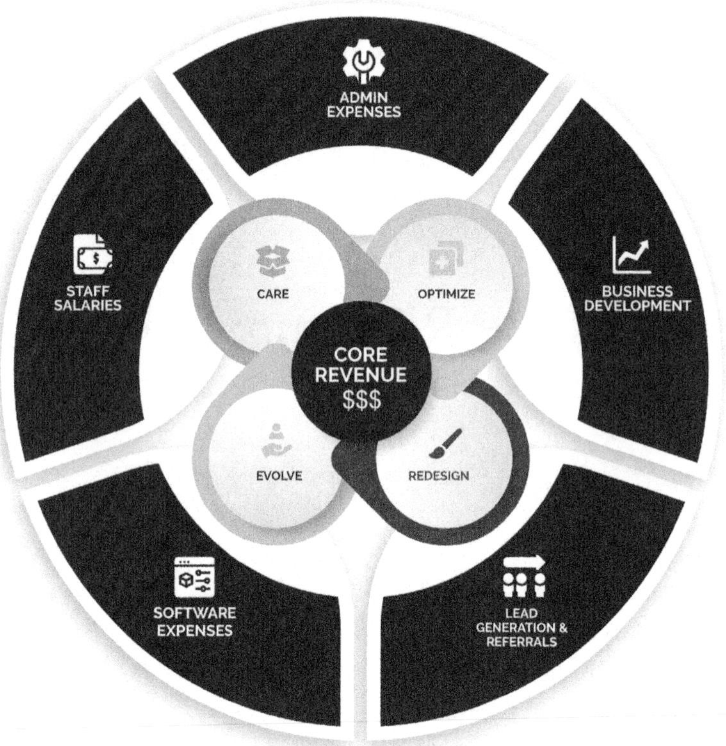

When I talk about your CORE list of clients, I'm referring to subscribers to your Care product, which I will discuss in this chapter. Your CORE list of clients is the group that engages in a revenue relationship. Be aware that just because someone once purchased a product or service does not mean they are a CORE client. They didn't engage in a relationship; they engaged in a transaction. A CORE list of clients is those that have subscribed to some recurring revenue product or productized service.

Begin to think of your revenue stemming from a recurring revenue offer and building a substantial monthly income that supports the entire business. Anyone you've worked with in the past can quickly become someone on your CORE list of clients.

This section of CORE Revenue will follow the same pattern as CORE Calibration. The C stands for Care as executed in a Care productized service. Then there are the offerings that Optimize that Care product. Next is how you help your CORE list of clients Redesign. Lastly will be how you can evaluate your clients to Evolve so they grow toward their goals.

Creating your Care product

Just like in calibration, C stands for Care. In CORE Revenue, however, it's how Care relates to a productized service, the center of your wheel. To properly incorporate The Revenue Relationship, you need a gateway product to begin the relationship between you and your client. An ideal Care offering provides the client with an ongoing productized service and is the foundation of that revenue relationship.

There are a few requirements for a Care product. By defining what this looks like, it'll be easier for you to craft what that product will be in your business. Even if you already have one, now is the time to tweak it. You can always tweak to adjust a Care product to your clients and your business at any stage. As we dig into what these Care products share across different industries, you will notice some fundamentals that make them suitable for recurring revenue.

If at any time you need more insight into how this relates to different businesses, view the Index of CORE Revenue at the end of this book.

As you read about these elements of a Care product, note that the qualities discussed discourage cancellations or churn. That is critical to the product being a gateway to The Revenue Relationship. Clients who cancel their "Care" product sever a relationship with you.

Having a product that encourages retention has everything to do with what you put inside that product. If we need to provide clients with something outside the Care product, then you will look at an Optimize product which I will get into in the next chapter.

1. Something the client or customer needs every month

The key to a Care product in The Revenue Relationship is that you're offering your client a productized service that supports them in their business. That productized service is something that they're going to need regularly. As we begin to craft our Care product, we want to consider the line items that our clients and customers need monthly.

In the website design and development industry, web professionals can offer website monitoring and maintenance as a Care product when working with a particular website platform. Website maintenance is a monthly need and helps support the business by monitoring and updating the website. Considering a website is a 24/7 sales tool, keeping it functioning, loading quickly, and safe from hackers supports the company, so their sales conversation online is uninterrupted.

Continuing with the website maintenance analogy, when I started offering that Care product of website maintenance in my web agency, we included website monitoring, updating, and backups that the client could feasibly do themselves. However, the expertise I brought to the table if something broke was worth more to our clients than what they would spend in terms of their time. For my website client to carry out the maintenance service themselves, they would have to spend a few hours every month following the industry trends and changes, recognizing what was wrong with their website, and figuring out how to fix it. My expertise saved them time and money. That is the winning formula of a Care product.

Care products can apply to any service-based business. Living in Arizona, we have scorpions that plague our home. A standard Care productized service here in the Southwest is to spray regularly for scorpions around our house. In addition, we have our lawn maintenance that takes care of our front and back yard every month. Both the insect and lawn companies support our home through their monthly product-service offerings, which saves my husband and me time. They also provide other services that build off first having this revenue relationship. I'll explore how they offer those services in the next chapter on Optimize.

Even though scorpion detouring and lawn maintenance fit a personal need, they don't directly help my business. For this reason, the relationship isn't as solid or loyal as it could be. If your business serves other businesses, there is a greater potential for growth with your Care product. The ideal Care product is one that directly supports them in making more revenue.

2. Something the client could do themselves

The easiest way to determine what to include in your Care product is to evaluate tasks that the client can do themselves but doesn't want to for reasons of time or expertise. We look to tasks the client could do themselves because it's an easy way to quickly evaluate the tasks they need to do and understand the value of getting them done.

Think about changing the oil on your car. Indeed, we could all do it ourselves, but it takes more time than we'd like - we have to get the materials, invest in disposing of the oil and absorb the risk of doing it wrong. For car enthusiasts, this is their wheelhouse, and they don't mind doing the task, but for the average car owner, the affordable price we pay a company outweighs the time and investment of doing it ourselves.

The same logic applies to a Care product. Clients who are very hands-on in their business and wear every hat often want to do everything themselves. It can be challenging to convince them to hand over the pieces of their business you can do for them monthly. Some clients want to save every penny and don't see any value in investing in you to help their business.

These clients are not the right Revenue Relationship clients. You want to look for the type of clients who, although they could do it themselves through time and resources, find value in the relationship enough to engage with your business.

When we look at the financial services industry, we see another example in monthly bookkeeping as a "Care" productized service. I could balance my books and categorize my transactions to know monthly expenses and income. However, I pay a company to balance my books for the same reason as the oil change in the car. The time I have to invest, the materials, and absorbing the risk of doing it wrong outweighs the cost of doing it myself.

For the financial services company I pay for, bookkeeping is only part of what they offer. Still, the monthly bookkeeping service is the initial Care product that begins my engagement with them. It's the gateway to a relationship, and now as a client, I can engage in other services from payroll to tax preparation.

So when thinking about crafting a Care product, focus on some of the daily, weekly, or monthly activities a client would have to do in their business they may not want or have the resources to do well. You must think across all clients you serve so your Care product is generalized enough to relate to everyone in your niche. Your Care product is the base productized service every one of your CORE clients subscribes to.

3. Something that ties you to the client or customer for invested interest in their growth or success

Creating recurring revenue from a list of CORE clients is most successful when the productized service directly contributes to the growth of their businesses. When your Care product does this, you're going to see an ability to scale, you're going to see incredible retention rates, and you're going to see a way to continue to optimize for more revenue.

That's because The Revenue Relationship balances their investment in you with you investing in their business. You do this with your time and expertise. Both of your businesses grow. It's the most honest approach to working with other business owners.

When we look at creating a Care product, we want to look at something that directly or indirectly grows your client's business and contributes to their success. That does not mean it has to be something that makes your client money. It can be as simple as freeing up time in their day so they have more time to spend on the growth of their business. It could mean offering peace of mind so they can turn their attention to other meaningful tasks. It could also mean protecting their investments by preventing anything from happening that would cost them money.

In understanding what frees time and what tasks to remove from their plate, you must put yourself in their shoes as a business owner. With the example of website maintenance, knowing what to include can be easily achieved by owning and operating a website yourself. By going through the steps of keeping a website up-to-date, you can evaluate the time needed to execute what will keep it secure and performing well.

If you need help determining what to include in your Care product, reach out to your clients and have a discussion. You want to ask the following questions: Is there anything we can take off your plate or your staff's plate on a daily, weekly, or monthly basis? What do you need help with to execute your chosen SMART goal?

What proactively protects your client from lost revenue can be challenging to stay on top of. Spending time following trends, news announcements, and updates to specific software can be burdensome for clients. If we go back to the bookkeeper example, my bookkeeper also offers CPA services. Since I don't have time or interest in following the US tax law changes, I'd rather give that responsibility to them.

If clients are investing in you monthly, you can follow these trends and news releases to anticipate what they need before they do.

4. Must follow a process to be profitable

You can only make something into a process once you first determine what to include in the productized service, which the previous points explored. Then and only then can you craft a repeatable process to deliver the productized service. Once it's repeatable, it can be profitable.

When we look at what classifies a Care product, we're talking about a fixed scope of work with a fixed process every month that doesn't vary from client to client.

When you have a well-defined process, you can predict the time to execute. Once time and resources are determined, you know exactly how much the Care product will cost. It's only by knowing these predictable variables that you're then able to make it profitable. How profitable? That truly depends on your industry, your expenses, the amount you need to invest in a team to execute, and any other factors that go into making sure your business is running within budget.

I prefer Care products to have a 60% profit margin or higher. I chose that number because a Care product's revenue should be the primary source of all your CORE revenue. At 60%+, the care product becomes worthwhile to execute and scale. We'll get into what additional revenue factors into that as well, but ideally, you want your Care product revenue to support the majority of the operating expenses of your business.

To keep a high profit margin and have your Care product be a fair price to your client, you need to have an airtight process that reduces unnecessary time and cost for execution. The price should be a good value compared to the time and expenses for the client to do it themselves or have their staff. That is also why you need to pay attention to what goes into the Care product and what is better reserved for an Optimize or Redesign product or service.

You can also achieve a fair price for the process by investing in well-trained staff. Whether in-house or outsourced, well-trained staff can handle and scale a process for multiple clients as long as it's airtight and well-defined. Additionally, software that offers bulk discounts and automation tools removes some points of human touch and drives down costs.

If you optimize your process enough, the cost of this Care product will decrease, and the profit margin will increase, all while staying a fair value for your client.

Care product in action

In the website design industry, the ideal product for a Care product is a "Website Care Plan." The website care plan is a recurring subscription product and is the gateway for the client to invest in the website professional to care for their 24/7 sales tool (their website).

Most websites cost thousands of dollars to create. A website can be taken down by the smallest of issues, like a car never changing its oil. Similar to a maintenance worker at a brick-and-mortar storefront or a building manager for a condominium, the web professional ensures that investment is protected and performs well for the client.

Using the case study of a Website Care Plan, I'll actionably apply the four steps above to outline how a website professional would craft their Care product.

What does the client need every month for a live website? For the management of their website, we're looking at updating their website software, monitoring the security, monitoring a fast performance, performing daily backups, executing necessary website content changes, and fixing bugs or errors that arise.

Is this something the client could do themselves? Absolutely. They or a person on their team could spend the time learning the steps to execute and pay the money for the necessary software needed to monitor. However, this website care is often just a distraction for the client and a burden to retrain staff to execute.

Web professionals often put too many tasks into a Website Care Plan. They don't apply the primary goal of the Care product, to take necessary tasks off the plate of their client in order to engage in a relationship. When website professionals stuff their productized service with non-essential items, they run the risk of a client not seeing the Care product as valuable. When the Care product serves as the base of the relationship you open a gateway to provide additional tasks through Optimize and Redesign services.

The concept of the Care product is to create a foundation for your CORE revenue as a recurring product that the client won't need to cancel. It should be vital for them to have regularly; a product that serves their basic needs.

Moving onto the next point, does the Care product of a Website Care Plan tie you to the client for invested growth in their success? 100%. In this example, a client needs a website performing and secure for the website professional to carry out any additional services: graphic design, SEO, online marketing, etc. If the website breaks or loads slowly, other services needed for growth can't be executed.

When considering what to add into your Care product, you must consider what makes for a good revenue relationship with the client. What is worth having them on your exclusive list of clients, and what is that price worth to them in taking care of their basic monthly needs?

Now, most clients need more than the basics, and that's where Optimize and Redesign (the following chapters) come in. Optimization in this Website Care Plan example would be services like search engine optimization, content creation, social media management, or pay-per-click marketing. Adding those optimizations into the Care product defeats the purpose of the foundational center product of your Care revenue. Web professionals that offer a wide variety of website services, including search engine optimization in a Care product, confuses the positioning. Once a client no longer needs search engine optimization or finds it unnecessary, it increases the chance of canceling the Care product.

Continuing with our Website Care Plan example of a Care product, we come to the "process for profit" question. At the time of this book, these plans with a basic scope of work can be a fair $99 a month value in the United States. The profit would need to be at $60 a month to be 60%. To stay within that budget, the website professional will need to find a way to execute the process with tools and automation.

If the client perceives their website as their 24/7 sales tool, investing in a Care product for their website performance and security becomes a no-brainer. With the Care product established, the client also recognizes the website professional as worthy of a revenue relationship,

Care product as the base of more revenue

The Care product is a gateway for the client to engage with your business. If done well, it becomes the base of your CORE revenue. The goal is retention: keeping clients on that Care product. Much of retention has to do with the scope of work of your Care product. You will achieve that goal if you apply the four principles in this chapter.

Keep in mind that the Care product is mutually beneficial. Clients benefit from getting on your exclusive list and having access to additional ways you can grow their business. These additions come in the form of Optimize and Redesign, the subjects of the following two chapters.

CHAPTER 8

CORE Revenue: Optimize

THE CARE PRODUCT IS THE FOUNDATIONAL COMPONENT OF YOUR CORE REVENUE. Without it, there is no relationship in which to offer additional items that will round out your CORE Revenue income. The limiting nature of the Care product scope of work is its strength. It means anything optional for monthly attention is a better fit for other productized services. The next stage, Optimize, involves what your client needs to improve their existing Care product and grow their business with you in additional offerings.

In CORE Calibration's Optimize, you needed to optimize your business with processes to grow. In CORE Revenue's Optimize, your client needs your help to grow with your services. Optimizations are best when they are additional recurring revenue subscriptions like your Care product. Because of their nature as offerings that may not apply to all clients or only to stages of business, Optimize productized services often have a higher chance of churn (cancellation). Since they go beyond the basic needs of Care and into areas that are motivated by reaching goals, they also come with higher ticket prices than your Care product.

Optimizations act as a "bolt-on" to your Care product, so if the client should cancel those MRR offerings, there is no threat to the Care product since it stands alone.

Optimizations moves your clients closer to their goals

If looking at this through the lens of The Revenue Relationship, the Care product takes care of the client's basic needs to sustain what they already have, while Optimizations move them forward toward their goals.

In this way, by offering more productized services to your clients, you should be motivated by what helps them rather than what additional revenue you can squeeze out of them. Optimize isn't a money grab from your CORE clients. When reframed with the mindset of a Revenue Relationship, you are offering optimizations because it's the only way to help your clients grow their business. If you keep The Revenue Relationship as the central focus when creating these productized services, you can be confident they will subscribe. The demand will be there because you started with a focus on your clients rather than the end goal of increasing your CORE Revenue.

The other reality is that only some of your clients will be ready to optimize their business. Your Optimize subscribers will fluctuate in number based on where your clients are in their business, their immediate goals, and how well they're doing financially.

When creating Optimization productized services, you want to follow principles similar to your Care product but more flexible, as these offerings are specific to goals and not as general as your Care product.

1. Packaged recurring revenue service that is goal oriented

Optimization products are perfect for goal-oriented results. They're typically higher-priced options than the Care product because they involve more time, tools, steps, and specialized expertise than the Care product.

They, like the Care product, should also be an ongoing service. The nature of it being recurring revenue benefits both you and the client. It means that you are committed and available every month to assist them toward their goals, and for you, it means that you will have the consistent revenue you need to perform.

When looking at what to package as a productized service, look at what you have done for clients in the past to achieve specific results. That can vary between business-to-business and client-to-client, so you have to look for what most businesses need to take your services to the next level.

In web design and development, perfect Optimize offerings involve monthly items like search engine optimization, pay-per-click ad management, content creation, and social media management packages, to name a few.

Each one of those pieces can be complementary to the Care product of maintaining and monitoring a client's website. However, maintaining and monitoring a client's website may not help them reach their larger goals, and that's the distinction between the two. As we discussed in the last chapter, a Care product can free up time or protect the revenue loss for your client. Optimize is the product that gets "added on" to grow your client's business in a way that they may not be doing themselves, have the skill to do themselves, or even *thought* to do at all. For this reason, you will have many Optimize products, yet one Care product.

Using the example of bookkeeping as a Care product from the last chapter, the ideal Optimize offerings would be monthly tax strategy or financial planning. Bookkeeping is a standard Care product that opens the door to relationships and increases trust. Monthly tax strategy and financial planning are additional services that help grow the business.

The best way to begin to craft what to include in your various Optimize products is by speaking with your clients to understand their goals. By determining where you can factor into achieving these goals, you can align your business to produce the means to make that happen. Keeping this as the focus for your Optimize products will allow you to create a suite of choices for your clients to continue a Revenue Relationship for success.

2. Should stand alone and complement other optimization products

Too often, I see people try to place Optimize services within their Care product because it creates a "big ticket" item. It's tempting to commit your client to a larger monthly bill rather than a series of add-ons. The problem with this is that the Care and Optimize products offer and achieve different things.

An Optimize offer is results-oriented. Yet, whenever you offer something that is results-oriented, you risk not producing enough results, not producing results fast enough, or underperforming. When any service is result oriented, you have a chance of clients cancelling that service. When you pair too many items in one big-ticket item, you give the impression that they work together. Clients who look to cancel will end up cancelling their entire relationship with you out of misunderstanding.

Even if the Care product and Optimize products don't get lumped together, it doesn't mean they don't complement one another. Think of all your productized services as building blocks toward a complete goal. There are multiple steps and multiple events that have to happen to bring someone to their destination. Make that journey visible through what you offer your clients.

Let's take the goal of increasing website traffic as an example. If someone wants to improve website visitors by 50%, a few things must happen to get them there. This goal is not a one-off service. To achieve more website traffic, they need an optimized website, search engine optimization, more content for search engines to index, and ads to direct traffic to their website from other places on the web.

Each of those are productized services that complement the complete goal of increasing website traffic. That is how Optimize products work best. As the expert, you should continue to discuss one particular goal. This way, your client is clear on how the relationship is working to achieve the results they want.

3. *Must follow a process to be profitable*

Just like a Care product, Optimize products need a process to be profitable. That means Optimize products must have a fixed scope of work. When offering Optimize products, keep in mind that this isn't something you're quoting specifically for a client with the scope of work and a price tag fluctuating for every client. If we are talking Optimize inside CORE Revenue, these are best as recurring revenue subscription products.

These productized services must be repeatable with a fixed scope of work and a process. If repeatable, then you can delegate them to a team. The only way for Optimize offerings to serve your CORE Revenue as profitable is to make sure you're building them in a way that sticks to a process.

Crafting Optimize products to be a fixed scope of work for recurring revenue takes work. The steps needed for your client to reach their goals can vary with specific businesses. If you focus on key pieces of every execution that are repeatable across most businesses you serve, the process will start to form.

For an accountant creating an Optimize product for tax strategy, it may not seem like it can have a repeatable process. Just because the principal accountant needs to execute the bulk of the value doesn't negate it from a process. A process for tax strategy as a productized service might involve an automated invitation to book the monthly call, a form to enter concerns for the month, and email reminders for the upcoming session. During the session, the accountant may have an assistant join or use a transcription tool to have staff complete the report and tasks on what the client needs to do.

Remember, the only reason why these are within a fixed scope is so you can have a repeatable process. The only reason you need a repeatable process is so you can make it profitable. You can fine-tune the steps with automation to remove much of the human touch during a process. That will prevent bottlenecks, increase efficiency, increase the speed at which it's executed, and will, overall, increase profit.

Spend your time on the processes for your productized services. The better the process, the more automation you can include. The more it can be automated or delegated, the more profitable it becomes.

4. Is not a one-time, one-off service

The Care and Optimize products don't work with The Revenue Relationship if they are one-time, one-off services. These embody the principle of CORE Revenue as recurring revenue productized services. Quarterly or yearly offerings can qualify in certain situations but are less ideal than monthly.

A one-time, one-off service is often less profitable, more time-consuming, and more of a challenge to execute since processes fluctuate to clients' needs. The varying scope of work from one-time, one-off services requires more admin time for scoping, billing, task management, and other variables.

The Optimize products are productized services. They need to include the segments of what you would carry out in a one-off service, but not include the line items that cannot be repeated monthly.

How do you account for the varying differences in clients? You can account for unpredictable nuances with onboarding services, offboarding services, and various "tiers" to your products.

Think of your Optimize products like a highway. When merging onto a highway, cars must enter through an onramp, sometimes at different speeds. Once on the highway, they split into separate lanes for various reasons. When disembarking the highway, they choose other exits. All this to say, the highway is the same for all, headed in the same direction. It even has a speed limit that applies to all drivers, even within all those various conditions.

The best way to account for the differences your clients will need in your Optimize products is a one-time, one-off service such as an onboarding product, just like that highway onramp. With the onboarding product, you can bring your client "up to speed" by addressing what they need to complete before a monthly service. The onboarding process can even be a one-time proposal with a quote specific to them. You can even productize the onboarding product, accounting for specific client needs in a series of onboarding products.

Like different highway lanes, your Optimize products can have different tiers that provide more line items for faster or increased results. Often you'll see a three-tiered structure to these products with a Goldilocks and the Three Bears approach, meaning the middle plan is always "just right."

In taking a tiered approach, ensure you are accounting for the increased time, attention, and resources needed for the higher plans. When going back to the scope of work, focus again on goals. Determine what your clients need to get to their destinations faster or to increase the number of results, and you'll discover the varying line items of your three-tiered or two-tiered plans.

Lastly, your Optimize offerings must have an offboarding service just like an offramp. This is vital for a few reasons. You want your clients to be clear on what they are cancelling and prep them for a return should that be necessary. It's also an opportunity to showcase the results of your "highway" and how far they've come. An offboarding service can be a crucial strategy for clients to return to your Optimize products once they are in the next stage of their business.

Optimization products in action

When looking at Optimize products through the lens of the web design industry, these productized services are typically recurring subscription products for search engine optimization, social media management, online marketing, and content creation. All these examples share a very targeted goal-driven theme.

For a website client, the web professional will have their Care product (Website Care Plan) and optimize that by having the client also purchase an SEO Plan (search engine optimization). This package may get the client to their goals in the next six months. If something changes and shifts for the client, they may cancel their SEO Plan, but that decision shouldn't affect the Website Care Plan. That Care product is necessary for the relationship with the website professional and the business' 24/7 sales tool (their website).

When putting a client on an SEO plan, they will need to have their website in a place where they can benefit from a scaled-down, systemized monthly process for SEO. The onboarding process would require optimizing the entire website by updating metadata, descriptions, images, and links. This way, the ongoing process of SEO is just optimizing new content, continued link building, and assisting the client in analytics of what's working and what's not.

The client can only get to this stage of a productized monthly service if their entire website is ready to benefit from a monthly process of SEO. That onboarding process is critical for the optimized production of the SEO plan to work. The SEO plan cannot work if all your clients are in varying places with the status of their website. All clients have to be brought up to a level playing field (the speed on the highway) so that the line items included in a monthly service for SEO can achieve the results it needs to, and they can disembark at any time, should their needs change.

Returning to the example of the bookkeeping CPA, the accountant can only give tax strategy advice if the client's books are up-to-date and accurate. Only by having that Care product of bookkeeping can they provide Optimize services of tax strategy and financial planning.

Optimize to increase your CORE revenue

Optimize products increases your CORE revenue, the predictable revenue that supports your business every month. By getting a robust menu of the right Optimize products to offer clients who subscribe to a Care product, you are positioning yourself as someone who invests in your clients' success.

The danger of Optimize products is trying to sell too much. Clients will be confused about what you provide if they don't complement one another toward larger goals. Additionally, if you have numerous Optimize products, you'll have numerous processes. It's not a disaster situation. It just means you need a knowledgeable and well-trained team. By offering more, you may, in turn, profit less.

Keep your Optimize products as productized services that serve your clients' goals. Have them complement one another and tell a story about you as a company, what you specialize in, and why you're the right choice for your clients.

CHAPTER 9

CORE Revenue: Redesign

The Care and the Optimize products make up a significant portion of CORE Revenue. However, in a service-based business, there is still a need for one-off services (or projects) that don't fit into a productized service. These services fall into the "R" of CORE Revenue or Redesign revenue.

In CORE Calibration, you redesign your role and the business to accommodate growth. In CORE Revenue, our clients benefit from services that assist them in redesigning their business in a specific way. Redesign allows the freedom to address client needs with offerings that cannot be a productized service.

Redesign makes goals possible

Redesign revenue is essential to our CORE revenue as it flows from the relationship with our CORE clients and provides a range of fees based on what type of service-based business you are. These projects are possible because the client trusts you thanks to an established Revenue Relationship. Redesign services are similar to Optimize in that they should be goal-driven. Goals are specific to the client and achieved in one-off projects or services.

1. One-off projects just for the client

If you supply services for businesses, chances are you're working with clients who desire to increase revenue through productivity, efficiency, sales, or expansion. If you're redesigning your businesses in the mindset of a Revenue Relationship, you should expect to answer how you help them achieve those revenue goals. Offering just Care and Optimize products leaves money on the table and opens gaps in ways to support. For service-based businesses, it's unrealistic to assume that everything you offer can be a fixed scope of work, a recurring revenue product.

Many businesses can thrive on Care and Optimize products. Yet, when you understand how Redesign revenue fits into CORE Revenue, you will find its welcome place in your offerings.

I call this section of the CORE revenue "Redesign" because it happens after your client has engaged in business with you. In website design and development services, a client often begins the relationship with a website. That project would be outside of CORE Revenue. When your client needs that website changed, a.k.a redesigned, it falls into the CORE Revenue.

Like the redesign portion of the CORE calibration, you can only understand what needs to change after some time has passed. When we look at Revenue services versus Care and Optimize products, we need to know how flexible we can be with our scope of work.

Redesign services require conversations with the client, digging into needs, then presenting that one-off service in a quote or proposal. A Redesign service should be significantly more revenue than the monthly charge of a Care product or an Optimize product. Since the scope of work is specific to the client's needs, it also involves more time than a Care or Optimize product.

Knowing what to include in a Redesign revenue service comes down to the one-on-one attention you can give a client. If your client needs a specific scope of work, you're looking at a Redesign revenue service.

2. A process for Redesign to be profitable

Even though the Redesign offer isn't a recurring revenue product, this doesn't mean it shouldn't have a process. Like everything we explored before, if you don't have a process for an offer, making it profitable is very challenging.

The main difference is that your service offer involves various processes that combine to form a custom solution for each client. When looking to dial in on a set of processes for Redesign, take each line item of the offer individually.

In redesigning a website, there's a process for designing, receiving client feedback, applying client feedback, development, and delivery. These processes may involve boundaries that help them become processes like only offering two design passes for notes and changes. A process is also successful when software and automation work together to move the process forward.

Singling out the various line items for each one of the popular services you quote makes forming these processes easier. Take each line item and look for ways to make each step repeatable. For each piece, look for how the client tries to increase the scope and wrap boundaries around those deliverables.

As in the example above, we limited design notes and changes to two passes. That's an example of restricting the scope of work that favors a repeatable process. If the client needs a third pass of notes and changes, this is outside the scope of work and involves a change request allowing you to address an additional charge to stay profitable.

It is helpful to dial into your niche and who you serve best. If you don't know who your niche is, you customize everything for each client and risk profit as time and resources become unpredictable. Therefore take the time to make a process.

3. Something that improves the client's business

To better classify Redesign revenue, view it as projects that ensure the client reaches a new level through customized improvements. If they have been a client for a while, there is a history to review for opportunities to improve. It may involve applying a particular technology or a recent change in the marketplace to their business.

By singling out Redesign as something that will improve and elevate the client into a new phase in their business, you'll be able to see what type of client will be the ideal CORE client. The desire to improve a client's outcome may change who you want to attract to your CORE list.

Over the years, my CORE list of clients changed frequently. It wasn't that I fired clients, although I did. It was more that when I had to adjust what I was offering, whether with pricing or removing services, the list naturally pruned itself.

Often shifting this focus to The Revenue Relationship illuminates the clients who have been leeches to the business, draining it in all the wrong ways. Look for the type of clients that are going to be the best type of clients for you.

Edit your client list through the lens of who you can help the most. When we start our businesses, we tend to take whatever business comes through the door, and not everyone is the type of client we want to serve. By making one of the levels of CORE Revenue Redesign, we look for businesses that can grow. You will likely end up attracting these types of businesses if "How can I help you grow?" is your conversation with current clients and prospects.

Redesign revenue in action

Redesign revenue is quite simple to define in the web design industry as it's typically website redesigns. Redesign projects in the web design industry range from redesigning a homepage to an entire website. However, the concept of the service can also apply to many projects, like calibrating someone's social media accounts, setting up course offerings on a learning management platform, or taking the time to redesign the client's Google Business listing.

In our previous examples of an accountant, preparing taxes could be classified as Redesign revenue. It's a one-off service that helps the business achieve its compliance goals and, hopefully, a refund.

For the lawn maintenance service previously discussed, reconstructing a fence, designing and erecting a garden, or building an outdoor patio are all worth Redesign service offerings.

As clients subscribe to a Care product, you form a relationship that leads to additional work. Whether designing a website or working on taxes, you are achieving a one-off task possible because of the Care and Optimize products. In the last chapter, we spoke about onboarding and offboarding services. You can make these Redesign revenue. As long as one-off services are for an existing client, you can place them in this category.

Redesign projects can be small-ticket items with few steps. In web design, edits on a website to fix issues or repair what's not working is Redesign revenue. Anything that takes what the client had before they get to you, or anything that they've done over time with you that you correct, fix, repair, or improve, is essentially Redesign revenue.

Redesign revenue is CORE Revenue

As much as we want to operate as a productized service business and strive for as much recurring revenue as possible, the goal should always be The Revenue Relationship and helping your client achieve. What can't be limited to a productized service often falls into Redesign, allowing the CORE Revenue model to include those one-off customized services.

Only through those types of services can we focus and narrow into our clients and really begin to offer them our talent and expertise on a personal level. You want to ensure you're working with the clients your business can grow and deliver results for. That is why making sure the types of clients you have in your CORE list is fundamental to making sure that this methodology works.

We must remember that our CORE list of clients is part of The Revenue Relationship. If you just set up your clients with a Care product and one or two Optimize products, then set and forget, you do them and yourself a great disservice.

Redesign revenue is a part of CORE Revenue for a reason. It's revenue from your CORE list of clients already on a Care product and possibly on Optimize products as well. Consistently consider your clients as those who benefit from your expertise, specialties, and knowledge. Thinking in this way changes what you offer, building a resilient business with loyal clients.

CHAPTER 10

CORE Revenue: Evolve

The final piece of CORE Revenue may not directly connect to income, but it's unquestionably essential. Evolve is the analytic and proactive efforts of your client's journey through Care, Optimize, and Redesign. As Evolve in CORE Calibration assists in getting your business to the next level, Evolve in CORE Revenue helps get your client to the next level.

To break it down as a cycle, in CORE Revenue, the client starts with a Care product to begin the relationship and trust. Then, based on their goals, they engage in an Optimize product. To further achieve the goal, they contract a one-off service with a Redesign offer. At the end of that cycle is Evolve. Evolve is the step we take to evaluate whether they achieve the goal of Optimize and Redesign. If the client isn't engaged in an Optimize product or any Redesign, review whether the Care product is enough for the client.

Reviewing the CORE diagram below, view how Evolve helps get the wheel of CORE Revenue back to Care. That is because business growth is a constant cycle of Care - Optimize - Redesign. Everything done for a client needs to be reviewed to motivate potential change for further growth.

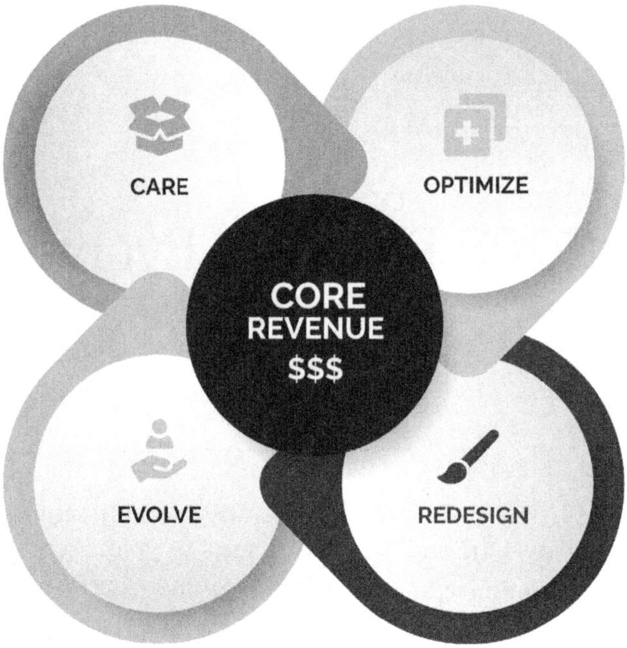

Evolve is proactive

Evolve is a proactive piece of the CORE Revenue model and positions you as the expert. Without Evolve and the view of CORE Revenue as a cycle, the client determines what they need from you. When you focus on The Revenue Relationship, you help take that burden from the client, setting out to answer questions proactively with Evolve.

With the external and internal variables of life and business, goals change. That is why the cycle of CORE allows for a journey through each level on a repeated basis. Evolve keeps the flow of CORE going and assures we are moving in the right direction with the client toward their goals.

In the CORE Revenue model, Evolve is like a pause to check in. It can be as simple as a phone conversation, an email report, or an internal review of a client's history. Evolve is the measurable part of CORE Revenue and a way to monitor your clients' progress so you know how to adjust your offerings to them.

1. Begin with the SMART goals

In CORE Calibration, I had you set SMART goals for your business. Your clients also need SMART goals for the services you provide for them.

As a reminder, SMART is an acronym for specific, measurable, achievable, realistic, and time-bound. Even though you may not be a business consultant for your client, you're certainly trying to help them achieve a specific result through your products and services. Depending on your business, you don't even have to disclose SMART goals to the client. They can be internal and just between your team for what you want to see achieved for the client.

To be clear, you aren't setting SMART goals for their business, just for what you deliver. If you offer websites, a SMART goal may involve traffic performance. If you provide accounting services, a SMART goal may be financial solvency. If you offer social media management, a SMART goal may be an increase in social followers.

If you serve a niche, shared SMART goals become much easier to measure and improve upon. For social media management, a SMART goal to have more followers on a specific social platform may need to be revised because that platform has changed its algorithm. Taking the time to measure one client's SMART goal will, in turn, give you new opportunities for your other clients.

Evolve interweaves with all the pieces of CORE Revenue. It doesn't have to be its own stage but instead can occur at all CORE Revenue areas.

A Care product may include a monthly report that highlights a SMART goal. Evolve included in that Care product helps find any low-hanging fruit while keeping the bigger picture of the client's needs in sight.

With Optimize products, interweaving Evolve with SMART goals ensures the product achieves what they need, increasing retention rates. Secure SMART goals for clients within all your recurring revenue productized services.

2. Evaluations on a monthly, quarterly, or yearly basis

To view Evolve as a stage in CORE Revenue, set aside monthly, quarterly, or yearly evaluations of your client's progress. Evolve as a stage can take the form of a report, a strategy session, an in-person meet-up, or a KPI Dashboard that your team or theirs reviews.

A business that embraces Evolve is one looking to generate continued revenue from its CORE list of clients. On the opposite spectrum, business owners spending more time outward focused on lead generation rather than nurturing the clients they already have will skip over the Evolve stage. By not taking this breath in this CORE Revenue cycle, they will lose out on what to offer their clients and miss potential revenue.

Spend time setting up reports and dashboards through automation efforts to make this stage easier to access and talk about with your clients. Evolve does not have to be something you reference regularly.

Evolve works best when it's reviewed or seen within the context of evaluating changes or pivots after a set period of time.

Reaching out to discuss reports and numbers with your clients on what has transpired with the Care product or the Optimize products (or even the Redesign) is a step you're taking in The Revenue Relationship. By recognizing the stage of Evolve, you affirm that you invest in your clients' success. In return, they trust you to offer them what they need in their business.

3. Leverage automation for evaluations

Evaluations do not have to be manual. I encourage anyone following the CORE revenue to leverage software and automation with minimal human touch, so this area of CORE stays profitable.

An abundance of software is available online that, depending on the industry, can measure anything and provide automatic reports. To properly execute this and have it become an integral part of your CORE Revenue, you will need to invest in the right tools to implement.

As discussed in the last point, you don't have to deliver reports in a way that encourages a personal one-on-one connection every time. Having a dashboard that your client can view can present statistics and updates for the clients to determine their own evaluation and move forward with your suggestions automatically.

Yet, in my experience, most clients are not as consumed with evaluating how well our services have been doing for them as we are. If you're doing a good job delivering your Care product, your clients will typically trust you and not even need valuation from a report. Evolve is more than proving you moved the needle. It's also about when you don't move the needle and need a new strategy.

I often see business owners avoid the Evolve stage because they feel providing evaluations will be time-consuming or illuminate poor results. Evolve serves to aid the retention of your clients, direct to an Optimize product, or make a case for a Redesign. Take the time to think out a systematic process for delivering reports that will save you the headache of doing many pieces of Evolve manually.

4. Should include call-to-action items

When we talk about reports, dashboards, metrics, and analysis, we want to avoid dumping data on our clients. That's not the point of this piece of CORE Revenue. Evolve is about maturing to the next level. What good is data if it's not actionable?

With your expertise, it's up to you (your team or an AI) to interpret and put data into action items. These action items then translate to Redesign Revenue or even another Optimize product.

Potential clients want to see you have solutions to their problems. Proving this is the most challenging stage of lead conversion. However, once converted and on your CORE list, clients' motivations change as they value your understanding of problems. They will often ask, "Tell me what I need to do," or in some cases, "Tell me what I need to pay you to do this for me." CORE clients want simple, straightforward steps from you, the expert.

These action items inside evaluations don't have to be something you offer. Feel free to provide action items that may require another company or service outside your offerings. Evolve is meant to move the client forward. Clients will have difficulty seeing the point if you only deliver data and no action items.

Again, this doesn't have to be as frequent as it sounds. Putting this stage after Care, Optimize, and Redesign is purposeful. I want to frame Evolve as something that happens when you've developed a relationship with the client, spent some time on other solutions, and have a better understanding of what they need.

Action items may not be clear in your first few months with a client. There's no need to rush. Just make sure you eventually take your CORE Revenue client into the stage of Evolve. Embrace the principle that you must evaluate to move them forward.

Evolve revenue in action

Now, Evolve can be revenue-generating with strategy sessions and KPI reports as paid services. Evolve can stand independently to generate earnings for our CORE Revenue.

In the website maintenance example from previous chapters, let's explore what a client will need to get them ready for the Care product of monthly maintenance. An onboarding service involving cleaning up their website and executing development to get them to that "on-ramp" and onto the highway of website care is a viable productized service. It's an excellent opportunity for Evolve to be the starting point instead of Care.

The website professional can run the website through an evaluation and review any low-hanging fruit or potential long-term issues as the onboarding service. The paid service becomes necessary for the website to be ready for the Care product. This Evolve stage fits nicely into Evolve as revenue and becomes the starting point of the CORE Revenue cycle.

When Evolve is an equal piece of the CORE Revenue, earnings continue to grow. Without Evolve, you are simply maintaining your client at one stage, with no focus on improvement and leaving money on the table.

Evolve accounts for improvement and growth

There is always room for improvement as industries and technology change. It's challenging to keep up with all the daily news and transformations. It's even harder for your client. Keep yourself educated and listen to the whispers of change related to your niche. As changes come, you can add these as areas of focus when you look to Evolve your client.

By investing in Evolve with evaluations, analysis, and growth suggestions for your client, you are likely doing more than other businesses in your industry. It's easy to operate in the status quo, so competitors will live in that space and do the minimum.

The Revenue Relationship asks more of you. It challenges you to think of ways to help your client and evolve them to the next level. In turn, you create more CORE Revenue for your business. This exchange becomes an equal trade. If your client's business is evolving, they are naturally more competitive and profitable, hopefully earning more revenue. They return to you for more solutions in which you provide more products and services. That is The Revenue Relationship.

CHAPTER 11

Taking Action with the CORE Methodology

NOW WE COME TO THE FUN PART: PUTTING EVERYTHING YOU JUST READ INTO ACTION. I began this book with the promise that you could transform your business with what you already have to be more profitable and resilient. The challenge now is inspiring you to take action. Taking action is hard, so this section and the following chapters will attempt to make this as easy as possible. You will see results if you follow the prompts, fill in the blanks, and learn from the examples.

The best advice I ever received on taking action I got when I returned to my business after a three-month maternity leave. Nothing is more overwhelming than getting back to serving clients while trying to keep a tiny human alive. I was operating on little sleep and had to shift my schedule to allow for phone calls, emails, and project management while still having children at home.

The advice that changed everything was from my mother. Cutting through my exhaustion and desperation, she encouraged me to "just focus on getting one thing done today." That is excellent advice for two reasons. The first is that we set too high expectations for ourselves. The task list we give ourselves is often double or triple what we would give to someone else. If only one item from the CORE Action Plan is on your list to complete that day, chances are you will do it.

Getting just one thing done today is also great advice for the small win, the feeling of accomplishment. If you check that box, it means you move forward. You'll be encouraged to keep going.

With the "getting one thing done a day" framework, I've broken down the action plan into days and weeks. You don't have to take it at this pace. You could go much faster. Yet, by setting expectations in this way, I'm hoping I can keep you motivated, and that at the end of a financial quarter, you've calibrated and created your CORE Revenue, revolutionizing your business.

Download the Workbook

The following two chapters lay out a Calibration and Revenue action plan. These action plans pairs with a printable PDF workbook available for download at therevenuerelationship.com. Use the step-by-step prompts in the actions plans, along with the workbook, for guided implementation.

Download the workbook, print it out and keep it on hand when you go through the action plans. If you reach a roadblock because you can't make a decision or need time to brainstorm, I encourage you to keep pushing through. Just put something down on the paper and move on. Any action is better than inaction. Analysis paralysis is real. If you overthink, you risk getting nothing done. The beauty of these action plan worksheets is that they are just your thoughts! Nothing is set in stone. Everything is fluid. You can revisit your answers in the worksheets as you implement to change, add, or delete.

Kira, the Web Agency Owner

Before we jump into the action plans, I want to showcase the application of The Revenue Relationship through the story of a web agency owner implementing CORE Calibration and CORE Revenue in her business. I've worked with thousands of web professionals, and this story is a blend of three web professionals I know blended into one journey. Following "Kira's" journey below, I hope it will inspire you to dig in and transform your business.

Kira's main issue in her web agency is revenue predictability. She started as a freelancer working for other marketing agencies, but when her skill set improved, side jobs for clients outside the marketing agency proved she could make much more with less stress.

After two years of working for the marketing agency juggling her side jobs, she decided to set out independently. Since graphic design was always her skill, she focused heavily on language around redesign with beautiful designs.

Although Kira made more for designing and coding websites outside the marketing agency, her workflow was inconsistent. She would make $5K for one month and another month only make $2K. A few clients approached with requests to work on retainers since their needs frequently came every month. Kira created monthly retainers of five or 10 hours from this request. She thought it would be predictable income.

After a few months of offering retainers, Kira was so overwhelmed with the varied requests from those clients, that she felt she was working a full-time job for just a particular section of her client list. Other clients got ignored, and new website projects missed deadlines.

There were many times Kira wanted to quit and return to the marketing agency or pivot and only sell designs to vendor marketplaces. However, this meant acquiring a new target market and a considerable risk of starting another company.

Then Kira heard about The Revenue Relationship. She knew that was what she was missing. She had no relationship with her past clients, and the handful of clients on retainers had no scope of work or boundaries.

As Kira began to calibrate her business to incorporate The Revenue Relationship, she realized the first step, Care, was her most challenging. As she broke down everything she did in her business, she revealed no healthy boundaries, no clear niche, and services that lacked clear long-term goals.

Kira began by working on her niche. In the first few days of her CORE Action Plan, she worked out a target market of e-commerce clients that would appreciate quality design and need graphics on an ongoing basis.

Kira then worked out her top three services of website design, advertising graphics, and e-commerce website development. She realized that she enjoyed graphic design more than coding, so her role would be as the creative director and designer. That meant she would need to hire a developer onto her team to take over all coding and development work.

Over the next few days, she crafted the job description and hired a developer for her team. Her new developer, a former colleague, worked out processes for developing e-commerce websites while Kira worked out the process for the design stage. Additionally, Kira reworked her advertising graphics package to some campaign management.

A couple of weeks into her Calibration, Kira had a good handle on her SMART goal for the company. Kira wanted to get at least half her past clients onto a Care product in Q1. In Q2, she would aim to get at least 20% on an Optimize product. In Q3, with her new developer and capacity to redesign past sites, they would push some redesign to a few clients whose websites were outdated. In Q4, she would look to hire another graphic designer to expand into social media.

With her Calibration goals, Kira shifted focus to her productized services and offerings. Her Care product would be a Website Care Plan. Since her niche was e-commerce websites that sold physical products, she ensured her Website Care Plan included features that supported those websites. That meant some of Kira's past clients might not fit into the $250/m monthly service. So Kira developed a non-e-commerce plan for a lower price point only available to her legacy clients.

For Optimize, she crafted an ad/promotion package that would include graphics and campaign management.

For Redesign, Kira crafted a specific offer of landing pages for campaign and product launches. Landing pages, plus full website redesign, would operate within the new developer's tasks.

Since Kira's niche is e-commerce websites, she invested in a reporting system that created dashboards focused on sales and conversion. She also included quarterly strategy calls in her Website Care Plan, so check ins for clients could lead to growth opportunities.

Kira decided that for needs she didn't offer, she would work to build a list of trusted referrals. A referral list of colleagues relieves the pressure of having all the answers and allows Kira to feel she can help her e-commerce clients reach their goals.

Through CORE Calibration and CORE Revenue, Kira converted 80% of her past clients with her Care product, totaling $5,000/m in recurring revenue. In addition, five of those clients subscribed to her Optimize package at $500/m, increasing her recurring revenue to $7,500/m. Just through her initial outreach of new services, she lined up two website redesigns for $5,000 each.

By implementing The Revenue Relationship and CORE methodology, Kira went from unpredictable revenue and an uncontrollable flow of client requests to $100,000 a year in CORE Revenue.

Now, Kira can work with this CORE list of clients, ensuring they reach their goal while onboarding new clients and placing them on a Care product. Over time, Kira may expand her Optimize outcomes as clarity around her clients' need grows. For now, the CORE Revenue will allow her to educate herself on the market, increase her skill set, hire necessary support, and deliver quality work.

That's Kira's story. Now it's your turn.

CHAPTER 12

Action Plan: CORE Calibration

BY NOW, YOU KNOW WHY YOU WANT TO CALIBRATE YOUR BUSINESS AND WHAT YOU NEED TO CALIBRATE IT FOR, but what tasks do you need to complete?

> Download the PDF Workbook from therevenuerelationship.com and work through the step-by-step instructions below.

You don't need to work on everything all at once. In this action plan tasks can be broken down into smaller pieces. If you are busy, consider doing just one task a day If you have solid time to work on your business, take all of Care in one day, then Optimize, and so on.

Calibration: Care

To calibrate your business to establish Care at the center, address each task daily (for 30 min each) or all in one day for an accelerated path.

Task 1: Research and define who you serve (your niche)

Ideas - Review past clients for shared traits and projects you enjoyed.

Example: I build membership solutions for educators who teach or coach in person and online.

Task 2: List the common goals of that niche of clients

Ideas - Look for associations, Facebook groups, or other communities where your niche would hang out or educate themselves.

Example: My niche has a common goal of enrolling more students through search engine results. My niche also has a common goal of providing the best user experience to students to increase retention of their monthly programs.

Task 3: List how these goals translate to your products and services. Hint: Connect and group these products and services so they build on one another.

Example: I can help my niche reach its goals by providing membership websites built for community and instruction. Services and products can build on one another to offer ways to attract more students, like Membership Website Build (Service) -> Website Care Plan -> Search Engine Optimization Package.

Task 4: Outline touch points you execute (or plan to execute) for your clients (Example: Monthly SEO Report)

1.
2.
3.

Task 5: What boundaries will you construct for healthy client relationships (Example: Clients' customers contact the client only; we don't act as white label support)

1.
2.
3.

Reflection notes:
What is one thing you can change today to put CARE at the center of your business? Anything holding you back?

Calibration: Optimize

To calibrate your business with Optimize, address each task daily (for 30 min each) or all in one day for an accelerated path.

Task 1: Summarize the scope of work for your top three services

1.
2.
3.

Example: Membership websites will include a discovery phase, a design phase, a development phase, and then a launch. Two sets of revisions by the client are included in each phase before launch. The client will receive the design files and website on their server after the final payment.

Task 2: Draw a diagram/flowchart of the processes for one of those services

Task 3: Now take your diagram and identify points in the process that can be 1) automated, 2) delegated, 3) outsourced

Task 4: Detail the team roles in your business. Then write a summary of their job descriptions. If you don't have a team, we'll address your role in the next section.

Example: The graphic designer is responsible for the flowchart of the websites, the design of all web graphics, photo retouching, and applying the client's notes and changes to the design. My graphic designer works part-time for a maximum of 20 hours a week.

Task 5: Write out what role you need to hire. Then draft job a description for that future hire.

Reflection notes:
What is one thing you can change today to OPTIMIZE your business? Anything holding you back?

Calibration: Redesign

To calibrate your business with Redesign, address each task daily (for 30 min each) or all in one day for an accelerated path.

Task 1: Chronicle your day-to-day tasks

Example: Check emails from clients, respond to emails, run payroll, check tasks for employees, draft sales proposals, etc.

Task 2: Describe your role in your business as if you were hiring someone to replace 100% of what you do

Task 3: List three tasks you want to remove from your day and what or who will take them (Example: Payroll, outsource to accountant/CPA)

1.
2.
3.

Task 4: List potential new products or services that could become CORE Revenue to revisit in the CORE Revenue Action Plan (Example: Google Ad Management)

1.
2.
3.

Task 5: Draft an "announcement" email for your clients to reposition your role with them (and the addition of new team members if applicable).

Reflection notes:
What is one thing you can change today to REDESIGN your business? Anything holding you back?

Calibration: Evolve

To calibrate your business with Evolve, address each task daily (for 30 min each) or all in one day for an accelerated path.

Task 1: Define your number one SMART Goal for your business

Example: I plan to convert 10 clients onto an SEO Package Optimize product within six months.

Task 2: Establish what you will use to measure this goal

Example: Automation from the e-commerce sign-up page that will input data to my client spreadsheet on the date of outreach and subscription start date.

Task 3: List the top three tasks you must complete to achieve this goal (Example: Create an e-commerce sign-up page for SEO package)

1.
2.
3.

Task 4: List out the Key Performance Indicators for your business (Example: Retention % of clients on a CORE care product)

1.
2.
3.

Task 5: Research the software, SaaS or system you will use to visually access these KPIs for reports about your business.

Example: I will use the sales pipeline feature in Active Campaign to build a central business Kanban board.

Reflection notes:

What is one thing you can change today to EVOLVE your business? Anything holding you back?

CHAPTER 13

Action Plan: CORE Revenue

WITH A BUSINESS CALIBRATED FOR CARE, OPTIMIZE, REDESIGN, AND EVOLVE, YOU ARE READY TO ESTABLISH YOUR CORE REVENUE. Take your download of PDF Workbook from therevenuerelationship.com and work through the next section CORE Revenue with the step-by-step instructions below.

Download the PDF Workbook from therevenuerelationship.com and work through the step-by-step instructions below.

Remember, you don't need to work on everything all at once. To make implementing easier, break it down into smaller pieces. Consider doing just one task a day. If you have more time, take all of Care in one day, then Optimize, and so on.

CORE Revenue - Care

To create CORE Revenue with a Care product, address each task daily (for 30 min each) or all in one day for an accelerated path.

Task 1: List what you will include in your Care product or productized service. (Example: Website software updates)
1.
2.
3.
4.
5.

Task 2: Review you list of clients, their history, and project details. List your favorites and their projects to better understand ways for productization.

Ideas: Evaluate and edit your client list based on your niche, who would subscribe to a CARE product, and who is not an ideal client moving forward.

Task 3: List out what to include in a simple sales page for your Care product along with what you will use for processing payments.

Ideas: Don't overthink your setup. Go with a reliable payment processor that can take recurring payments and integrate them with a website you already have.

Task 4: Draft the email to introduce the Care product to your clients.

Task 5: Now build the sales page and send the email outreach to your client list to convert them to your Care product.

Ideas: You don't have to immediately send it to your entire list. Choose a segment of clients you think will convert well and start there. Positive responses will give you the confidence to send it to the rest of the list.

Pushing through roadblocks:
The sales page doesn't need to be perfect, just functional. Don't get hung up in small design details, "push the button" and take action.

CORE Revenue - Optimize

To create CORE Revenue with Optimize products, address each task daily (for 30 min each) or all in one day for an accelerated path.

Task 1: Brainstorm the different ways you could help Optimize your Care clients along with the goal each achieves (Example: Search Engine Optimization. Goal - Higher ranking for a top keyword)
1.
2.
3.
4.
5.

Task 2: Write the scope of work for one of those potential Optimize offerings.

Task 3: Now draw a diagram/flowchart of the Optimize product's process. Note what can be 1) automated, 2) delegated or 3) outsourced.

Task 4: Draft the email to introduce the Optimize product to your clients

Task 5: Set up the product for purchase and email outreach to your client list to convert them to your Optimize product

Ideas: Like with the Care product, you don't have to send it to your entire list immediately. Choose a segment of clients you think will convert well and start there. Positive responses will give you the confidence to send it to the rest of the list.

Pushing through roadblocks:
If you don't have a clear process, propose working with one client on this offering for a significantly reduced price. Use that time to develop the workflow and how much time/resources it takes to properly price it.

CORE Revenue - Redesign

To create CORE Revenue with Redesign services, address each task daily (for 30 min each) or all in one day for an accelerated path.

Task 1: List the top Redesign offerings, one-off products, or services (Example: Design and development of landing pages)

1.
2.
3.
4.
5.

Task 2: List the processes for you top (or most profitable) Redesign offer.

Example: Schedule call with client -> scope out the work -> send quote for agreement -> mockup landing page in flowchart software -> get approval from client -> design landing page.

Task 3: Review your client list and decide which clients would benefit for one of your redesign services.

Task 4: Draft an email to schedule a call with those clients, pitching the benefits of a redesign.

Task 5: Send the email outreach to a select segment of clients to convert them to your Redesign offer.

Tip: This should only be to a handful of clients. It should also be a soft pitch to schedule a time to discuss, so you can better tailor the redesign to them.

Pushing through roadblocks:
If you are having problems finding quality clients among your list, use the Redesign offer to convert them into a quality client. Determine what qualities, features, or business elements they need to be a client you can help, then work backwards from there.

CORE Revenue - Evolve

To move CORE Revenue forward with Evolve, address each task daily (for 30 min each) or all in one day for an accelerated path.

Task 1: List a common SMART goal your clients have. (Example: Convert 10% of visitors to the website to schedule a consultation within six months)
1.
2.

Task 2: List what you could you use to measure this goal.

Task 3: Determine what software, SaaS, or systems you could use to deliver reports or dashboards for strategy sessions. Then list what needs to be included in these reports or dashboards.

Task 4: Draft the email introducing your Evolve solution to your clients, like scheduling a strategy session or providing a link to a dashboard.

Task 5: Set up your Evolve solution then send the email to your clients.

Tip: Create a sample dashboard if this is an upsell for clients to pay for. If it is already included in your Care product, create the dashboards, and email the clients with their links.

Pushing through roadblocks:
If you are finding your clients' needs are all over the place, and no one Evolve solution fits, then just focus on a segment of your clients that can make this stage work. Then focus on acquiring more clients like those. Eventually you will build a healthy list of the types of clients you can serve best and fit nicely into the cycle of CORE Revenue.

CHAPTER 14

Finding Value in The Revenue Relationship

AS YOU PUT THESE PRINCIPLES INTO EFFECT, YOU WILL EVENTUALLY HIT SOME STUMBLING BLOCKS. However, if you find value in establishing The Revenue Relationship, you can figure out a way around those blocks. To assist, I decided to close out by outlining a few of the most common stumbling blocks business owners have in CORE Calibration and CORE Revenue: letting go, lead generation, and overwhelm.

Back to basics

Before jumping into those common problems, let's review the basics.

The Revenue Relationship works when applied to a client-focused service-based business, especially in the B2B world of helping companies grow. If you only provide products, you only deal with customers, not clients. These strategies work best with productized services and one-off projects for clients.

CORE Revenue allows you to take what you make from your CORE list of clients and support all the areas of your business from staff salaries, business expenses, outward lead generation, and admin expenses. That is how your business becomes resilient. If you don't work out each step of CORE, your wheel will be weak.

Every part of CORE Revenue services has a purpose. Deciding you don't need Optimize or Redesign may result in low CORE Revenue and the inability to support your business expenses.

CORE Revenue builds over time. As you shift to this model, your CORE Revenue will be low, but as you communicate to your clients your new style of working, you will see growth, more referrals, and more satisfaction among your clients.

What you need to offer and how your business looks will change over time. CORE Revenue is the wheel of the car that supports you moving forward. It allows you to improve the business processes for better profit and restructure offerings to what your niche of clients want every time you Evolve.

Letting go and being a better boss

As business owners, we constantly adapt to external factors and unexpected roadblocks. What may have worked a few years ago could flip at any moment and cause stress, frustration, and burnout. What if that roadblock is you?

An unintended crux of reading this book and applying the CORE methodology is discovering that you need to become a better boss. I don't mean a better boss to employees, although I'm sure that applies, but a better boss to yourself.

CORE Calibration shows you strategies and a mindset that helps you build boundaries, processes, and principles that give you the kind of business you want. To do that, you have to let go. If you don't let go, you will get stuck in a stressful business.

Yes, you can find freedom with a CORE list of clients. To embrace that freedom, you must let go of the tasks overtaking your role (Redesign), let go of the control to execute every piece (Optimize), and let go of people pleasing by staying strict with the scope of work in your Care product.

Letting go is challenging when your business is everything. Try taking a step away from your business with a vacation, a long tech-free weekend, or even a weekday off doing something you love. It will feel like coming up for air and may offer you the distance you need to finally agree to let go of critical pieces that will let CORE work its magic.

Lead generation within the CORE methodology

In this book we explored the strategy of "turning inward." We could invest in a relationship with our clients that, in turn, invests in us. The productized services we offer exhibit that trust since they are recurring revenue products, and yet, there's still freedom to engage in larger projects and evaluations within the CORE methodology. What about lead generation and outward sales when you don't have a list already?

This book is not abandoning the outward sales approach altogether. Lead generation and external sales are essential for growth. Yet, you don't want to scale something that isn't profitable, optimized, and ready to be scaled.

By all means, reach out and execute effective lead generation to acquire new clients. Do so, however, once you have a CORE Calibrated business with a system of CORE Revenue, even if that means just two or three clients. Then you can put new clients into that model for tremendous scale.

Once you have The Revenue Relationship and CORE Methodology in place, I recommend doing lead generation with your Optimize offerings and Redesign services. The Care product is essential, but lead generation is about selling results, and a Care product alone can be weak for outward sales since the relationship needs to be proven. If you include Care in your advertising, pair Care and Optimize or Care and Redesign as you lead generate. When doing so, all language should be around benefits and results for your clients.

Remember that you have yet to prove your end of the relationship in cold outreach. You must work on an initial project together to earn that trust. If using the CORE Methodology in lead generation, chances are they will be nervous about a recurring revenue product out the gate, so start with a Redesign project or Onboarding offering and build that trust.

Overwhelm: Taking action by going step by step

This book is more than just theory. It's meant to get you to take actionable steps. To do this, you must push through the CORE Action Plans to implement changes in your business. Work through these steps diligently every day to chip away at adjusting with CORE Calibration and building CORE Revenue.

The longer you have been running your business, the harder it is to prune back what you offer. If this is your situation, be gracious in giving yourself more time to act on changes.

If you have a lot of clients acquired over many years, it helps to single out a handful of clients and start to implement with just that segment. That allows you the confidence to apply these offerings, processes, and boundaries to the rest of your list. It also allows you to test what will work before committing it to your entire list.

If you ever feel overwhelmed, it's always wise to scale down and implement something on a smaller scale. You may have to prove this is the right direction, so choose something that will give you the quick result you need to keep moving forward.

A new perspective

As you close out these pages with a new perspective on the relationship with your clients and how The Revenue Relationship can sustain your business, ask for accountability, share this book with others, or join one of our groups to discuss the concepts.

It does take time to build a business with processes and predictable income. The CORE Calibration and CORE Revenue can act as the blueprint. Pick this book back up whenever you feel you are getting off track or need to evolve to the next level. Cycle back through CORE Calibration and continue to expand your CORE Revenue offerings.

Apply the action plans, and you'll begin to get the initial revenue you need to motivate your changes moving forward. It's time to be more resilient. It's time for The Revenue Relationship to revolutionize the way you do business.

Index: CORE Revenue Examples

CORE Revenue works best when businesses serve other businesses (B2B) since the outcome is focused on results that benefit the client's bottom line. Examples of service-based businesses below showcase what Care, Optimize, Redesign, and Evolve offerings could look like in this context.

Additionally, at the end of this list are examples of companies that offer CORE Revenue to consumers (B2C). You'll see the difference and how the CORE cycle only continues based on consumer satisfaction since business growth is not the overall objective.

Business Types

Website Development
Care - website maintenance
Optimize - search engine optimization
Redesign - website redesign
Evolve - monthly reports and quarterly strategy session

Graphic Design
Care - blog and social media graphics
Optimize - ads graphics
Redesign - rebranding logo and style guides
Evolve - focus group for brand feedback

Digital Marketing
Care - pay-per click management

Optimize - search engine optimization or content creation
Redesign - landing pages
Evolve - analytics and sales reports

Social Media Marketing
Care - social posts
Optimize - comment monitoring or video creation
Redesign - edit and update social pages
Evolve - analytics and engagement reports

IT and Security
Care - tech support
Optimize - cloud services
Redesign - new systems and software setup
Evolve - internal review of systems

Financial Services
Care - bookkeeping
Optimize - payroll, financial planning, or tax strategy
Redesign - tax preparation, portfolio building
Evolve - previous tax review, business strategy

Personal Needs (B2C) Type

In the examples below, these companies serve needs that don't directly relate to business growth. For this reason, Evolve is based on customer satisfaction initiated by the consumer as feedback.

Landscaping
Care - lawn maintenance
Optimize - tree trimming
Redesign - landscape redesign, planting, building
Evolve - customer satisfaction feedback

Pest Control

Care - spray treatment
Optimize - different bug/pest
Redesign - changing exterior/ interior environment
Evolve - customer satisfaction feedback

Gym / Fitness Coach

Care - gym access
Optimize – group classes
Redesign - personal training
Evolve - customer satisfaction feedback

ABOUT THE AUTHOR

Kristina Romero began as a website developer creating websites for companies that included the Coca-Cola Company, Food Network, and Hollywood celebrities. Through her experience running an agency, she developed a passion for helping other website professionals grow their businesses and better serve their clients. Kristina has trained thousands of web professionals with content across the web through webinars and courses. With her training programs, Kristina has built a community where website professionals can discover quality instruction to increase revenue and improve client relationships.

Printed in Great Britain
by Amazon

20055151R00078